ESSAYS ON GREAT WRITERS

ESSAYS ON
GREAT WRITERS

BY

HENRY DWIGHT SEDGWICK

Essay Index Reprint Series

BOOKS FOR LIBRARIES PRESS
FREEPORT, NEW YORK

First published 1903
Reprinted 1968

809
Se 2 e
65519
April 1969

LIBRARY OF CONGRESS CATALOG CARD NUMBER:
68-29245

PRINTED IN THE UNITED STATES OF AMERICA

To

MY FATHER

CONTENTS

LOCKHART'S LIFE OF SCOTT

LOCKHART'S LIFE OF SCOTT [1]

I

IT is wholly fit that Americans should go
on pilgrimage to Abbotsford. A remem-
brance of virtue is there which we, at least,
cannot find at Canterbury, Lourdes, or Loreto.
There is but one comparable spot in Great
Britain, and that is on the banks of Avon;
but at Stratford, encompassed by memorials
of idolatry, surrounded by restoration and
renovation, harried and jostled by tourists,
the pilgrim wearily passes from bust to portrait, from Halliwell to Furness, from side-
board to second-best bedstead, with a sick
sense of human immortality, till his eye
lights upon the " W. Scott " scrawled on the
window-pane. If Walter Scott made this
pilgrimage, if his feet limped through the
churchyard of Holy Trinity, if he looked at
the ugly busts, if he, too, was elbowed by

[1] *Memoirs of the Life of Sir Walter Scott*, by John Gibson
Lockhart. Boston and New York : Houghton, Mifflin &
Co. 1902. 5 vols.

American women there, then welcome all, the
sun shines fair on Stratford again.

Abbotsford has discomforts of its own, but
there one has glimpses of Scott's abounding
personality. How wonderful was that personality; how it sunned and warmed and
breathed balm upon the lean and Cassius-
like Lockhart, till that sweetened man became
transfigured, as it were, and wrote one of
the most acceptable and happy books of the
world ; — a personality, so rich and ripe, that
nature of necessity encased it in lovable
form and features. In the National Portrait
Gallery is a good picture of Scott, large-
browed, blue-eyed, ruddy-hued, the great out-
of-door genius; one of his dogs looks up at
him with sagacious appreciation. There is
the large free figure, but what can a painter
with all his art tell us of a person whom we
love? How can he describe the noble career
from boyhood to death; how can he deline-
ate the wit, the laughter, the generosity, the
high devotion, the lofty character, the dog-
ged resolution, and the womanly tenderness
of heart? The biographer has the harder
task. A hundred great portraits have been
painted, from Masaccio to John Sargent, but

the great biographies are a half dozen, and one of the best is this book of Lockhart's.

As generations roll on, the past drifts more and more from the field of our vision; the England of Scott's day has become a classic time, the subjects of George III. are strangers of foreign habits; tastes change, customs alter, books multiply, and with all the rest the Waverley Novels likewise show their antique dress and betray their mortality; but the life of a great man never loses its interest. As a time recedes into remoteness, its books, saving the few on which time has no claim, become unreadable, but a man's life retains and tightens its hold upon us. It is hardly too much to say that Lockhart has done for Scott's fame almost as much as Scott himself. The greatest of Scotsmen in thirty novels and half a dozen volumes of poetry has sketched his own lineaments, but Lockhart has filled out that sketch with necessary amplification, admiring and just. What would we not give for such a biography of Homer or Virgil, of Dante or Shakespeare? But if we possessed one, dare we hope for a record of so much virtue and happiness, of so much honor and heroic duty?

Walter Scott is not only a novelist, not only a bountiful purveyor of enjoyment; his life sheds a light as well as a lustre on England. Of right he ought to be seated on St. George's horse, and honored as Britain's patron saint, for he represents what Britain's best should be, he, the loyal man, the constant friend, joyous in youth, laborious in manhood, high-minded in the sad decadent years, thinking no evil, and faithful with the greatest faith, that in virtue for virtue's sake. Every English-speaking person should be familiar with that noble life.

One sometimes wonders if a change might not without hurt be made in the studies of boys; whether Greek composition, or even solid geometry, — studies rolled upward like a stone to roll down again at the year's end with a glorious splash into the pool of oblivion, — might not be discontinued, and in its stead a course of biography be put. Boys should read and read again the biographies of good men. The first two should be the History of Don Quixote and Lockhart's Life of Scott. In young years, so fortified against enclitics and angles, yet unfolding and docile to things which touch the heart, would not the

boy derive as much benefit from an enthusi-
astic perusal of Lockhart's volumes as from
disheartening attempts to escalade the irregu-
lar aorist? It was not for nothing that the
wise Jesuits bade their young scholars read
the Lives of the Saints. Are there no lessons to be learned for the living of life?

Don Quixote and Sir Walter Scott look
very unlike, one with his cracked brain and
the other with his shrewd good sense, but
they have this in common, that Don Quixote
is an heroic man whose heroism is obscured
by craziness and by the irony under which
Cervantes hid his own great beliefs, while
Scott is an heroic man, whose heroism is
obscured by success and by the happiness
under which he concealed daily duty faithfully done. In the good school of hero-wor-
ship these men supplement one another, the
proud Spaniard, the canny Scot, great-hearted
gentlemen both. Our affection for them is
less a matter of argument than of instinct;
their worthiness is demonstrated by our love.
I cannot prove to you my joy in the month
of May; if you feel dismal and Novem-
brish, why, turn up your collar and shiver
lustily. The Spaniard is rather for men

who have failed as this world judges; the Scot for those who live in the sunshine of life.

English civilization, which with all its imperfections is to many of us the best, is a slow-growing plant; though pieced and patched with foreign graftings, it still keeps the same sap which has brought forth fruit this thousand years. It has fashioned certain ideals of manhood, which, while changing clothes and speech and modes of action, maintain a resemblance, an English type, not to be likened to foreign ideals, beautiful as those may be; we have much to learn from those great examples, but the noble type of the English is different. Sir Thomas Malory's Round Table, Philip Sidney, Falkland, Russell, Howard the philanthropist, Robertson the priest, Gordon the soldier, — choose whom you will, — have a national type, not over-flexible, but of a most enduring temper. The traditions which have gathered about these men have wrought a type of English gentleman which we honor in our unreasonable hearts. Our ideals are tardy and antiquated ; they savor of the past, of the long feudal past. We listen politely to the introducer of new doctrines of righteousness, of new principles of morality, and nod a cold approval, " How noble ! " " What a fine fellow ! " " Excellent man ! " but there is no touch of that enthusiasm with which we cry, " There ! there is a gentleman ! " A foolish method, no doubt, and worthy of the raps and raillery it receives, but it is the English way. Educated men, with their exact training in sociology and science, smile at us, mock us, bewail us, and still our cheeks flush with pleasure as we behold on some conspicuous stage the old type of English hero ; and we feel, ignorantly, that there is no higher title than that of gentleman, no better code of ethics than that of chivalry, rooted though it be on the absurd distinction between the man on horseback and the man on foot.

The great cause of Sir Walter Scott's popularity during life and fame after death is that he put into words the chivalric ideas of England, that he declared in poem, in romance, and in his actions, the honorable service rendered by the Cavalier to society, and so he stirred the deep instinctive affections — prejudices if you will — of British conservatism. He founded the Romantic

School in Great Britain, not because he was
pricked on by Border Ballads or by Götz von
Berlichingen, but because, descended from
the Flower of Yarrow and great-grandson of
a Killiecrankie man, he had been born and
bred a British gentleman, with all his poetic
nature sensitive to the beauty and charm of
chivalry. History as seen by a poet is quite
different from history as seen by a Social
Democrat ; and the Cavalier — if we may
draw distinctions that do not touch any
question of merit — requires a historian of
different temper and of different education
from the historian of the clerk or the plough-
man. The youth filled with rich enthusiasm for life, kindled into physical joy by a
hot gallop, quickened by a fine and tender
sympathy between man and beast, crammed
with fresh air, health, and delight, vivified
with beauty of April willows and autumnal
heather, is remote, stupidly remote perhaps,
from the scrivener at his desk, or the laborer
with his hoe. The difference is not just, it
is not in accord with sociological theories, it
must pass away ; yet it has existed in the
past and still survives in the present, and
a Cavalier to most of us is the accepted type

of gentleman, and "chivalric" is still the proudest adjective of praise. Of this section of life Sir Walter Scott is the great historian, and he became its historian, not so much because he was of it, as because he delighted in it with all his qualities of heart and head.

We still linger in the obscurity of the shadow cast by the Feudal Period ; we cannot avoid its errors, let us not forget the virtues which it prescribes ; let us remember the precepts of chivalry, truth-telling, honor, devotion, enthusiasm, compassion, reckless self-sacrifice for an ideal, love of one woman, and affection for the horse. For such learning there is no textbook like this Life of Scott. Moreover, in Lockhart's biography, we are studying the English humanities, we learn those special qualities which directed Scott's genius, those tastes and inclinations which, combining with his talents, enabled him to shift the course of English literature from its eighteenth-century shallows into what is known as the Romantic movement.

It is a satisfaction that America should render to Scott's memory the homage of this new edition of Lockhart with generous print,

broad margin, and that comfortable weight
that gives the hand a share in the pleasure
of the book and yet exacts no further service. What would the boy Walter Scott
have said, if in vision these stately volumes,
like Banquo's issue royally appareled, had
risen before him one after one, to interrupt
his urchin warfare in the streets of Edinburgh? But the physical book, admirable
as it is, equipped for dress parade and somewhat ostentatious in its pride of office, is
but the porter of its contents. Miss Susan
M. Francis, with pious care, excellent judgment, and sound discrimination, worthy
indeed of the true disciple, has done just
what other disciples have long been wishing
for. At appropriate places in the text, as if
Lockhart had paused to let Miss Francis step
forward and speak, come, in modest guise as
footnotes, pertinent passages from Scott's
Journal, and letters from Lady Louisa Stuart,
John Murray, and others. The Familiar Letters, the Journal, and many a book to which
Lockhart had no access, have supplied Miss
Francis with the material for these rich additions. The reader's pleasure is proof of the
great pains, good taste, and long experience

put to use in compiling these notes. The
editor's is an honest service honorably per-
formed. As a consequence — and perhaps I
speak as one of many — I now possess an
edition of Lockhart which, strong in text,
notes, and form, may make bold to stand
on the shelf beside what for me is *the* edition of the Waverley Novels. This edition
published in Boston — it bears the name
Samuel H. Parker — has a binding which
by some ordinance of Nature or of Time,
the two great givers of rights, has come to
be *the* proper dress of the Waverley Novels.
Its color varies from a deep mahogany to the
lighter hues of the horse-chestnut; what it
may have been before it was tinted by the
hands of three generations cannot be guessed.
This ripe color has penetrated within and
stained the pages with its shifting browns.
It is plain that Time has pored and paused
over these volumes, hesitating whether he
should not lay aside his scythe; he will travel
far before he shall find again so pleasant a
resting-place. This Parker edition used to
stand on a shelf between two windows, with
unregarded books above and below. On
another bookcase stood the Ticknor and Fields

edition of Lockhart, 1851, its back bedecked
with claymores and a filibeg, or some such
thing; the designer seems to have thought
that Scott was a Highland chief. But,
though exceeding respectable, that edition
was obviously of lower rank than the Parker
edition of the novels; be-claymored and fili-
begged it stood apart and ignored, while the
novels were taken out as if they had been
ballroom belles. In fact, there is something
feminine, something almost girlish, about a
delightful book; without wooing it will not
yield the full measure of its sweetness. In
those days we always made proper preparation — a boy's method of courtship — to read
Scott. The proper preparation — but who
has not discovered it for himself? — is to be
young, and to put an apple, a gillyflower, into
the right pocket, two slices of buttered bread,
quince jam between, into the left, thrust the
mahogany volume into the front pouch of
the sailor suit, then, carefully protecting
these protuberant burdens, shinny up into a
maple-tree, and there among the branches,
hidden by the leaves, which half hinder and
half invite the warm, green sunshine, sit
noiseless; the body be-appled and be-jammed

into quiescent sympathy, while the elated
spirit swims dolphin-like over the glorious
sea of romance. That one true way of reading the Waverley Novels poor Mr. Howells
never knew. He must have read them, if he
has read them at all, seated on a high stool,
rough and hard, with teetering legs, in a
dentist's parlor. He has had need to draw a
prodigal portion from his Fortunatus's purse
of our respect and affection to justify his
wayward obliquity toward Scott. I wish that
I were in a sailor's blouse again, that I might
shinny back into that maple-tree, in the company of Mr. Howells, with Miss Francis's
volumes of Lockhart (one at a time), to read
and re-read the story of Sir Walter Scott,
and feel again the joy which comes from the
perusal of a biography written by a wise
lover and edited by a wise disciple, with no
break in the chain of affection between us
and the object of our veneration. Perhaps
Miss Francis would do us the honor to take
a ladder and join our party. But youth and
jam and gillyflowers are luxuries soon spent,
and Miss Francis has done her best to make
amends for their evanescence. She has done
a public kindness, and she has had a double

reward, first, in living in familiar converse with Scott's spirit, second, in the thanks which must come to her thick and fast from all Scott lovers.

We might well wish that every young man and every boy were reading these big-printed volumes, adorned with pictures of our hero, of his friends, both men and dogs, and of the places where he lived. Let a man economize on his sons' clothes, on their puddings and toys, but the wise father is prodigal with books. A good book should have the pomp and circumstance of its rank, it should betray its gentle condition to the most casual beholder, so that he who sees it on a shelf shall be tempted to stretch forth his hand, and having grasped this fruit of an innocent tree of knowledge, shall eat, digest, and become a wiser, a happier, and a better man or boy.

II

Without meaning to disparage the Future, — it will have its flatterers, — or the Present, which is so importunately with us always, there is much reason with those who think that the home of poetry is in the Past. There our sentiments rest, like rays of light

which fall through storied windows and lie
in colored melancholy upon ancient tombs.
That which was once a poor, barren Present,
no better than our own, gains richness and
mystery, and, as it drifts through twilight
shades beyond the disturbing reach of human recollection, grows in refinement, in
tenderness, in nobility. Memory is the great
purgatory; in it the commonness, the trivi-
ality of daily happenings become cleansed
and ennobled, and our petty lives, gliding
back into the Eden from which they seem to
issue, become altogether innocent and beautiful.

In this world of memory there is an aristocracy; there are ephemeral things and long-
lived things, there is existence in every grade
of duration, but almost all on this great backward march gain in beauty and interest. It
is so in the memory of poets, it is so with
everybody. There is a fairy, benevolent and
solemn, who presides over memory; she is
capricious and fantastic, too, and busies herself with the little as well as with the big
things of life. If we look back on our
boarding-school days, what do we remember? Certainly not our lessons, nor the re-

bukes of our weary teachers, nor the once
everlasting study hour ; but we recall every
detail of the secret descent down the fire-
escape to the village pastry-cook's, where,
safeguarded by a system of signals stretching continuous to the point of danger, we
hurriedly swallowed creamcakes, Washing-
ton pies, raspberry turnovers, and then with
smeared lips and skulking gait stealthily
crept and climbed back to a sleep such as
few of the just enjoy.

This fairy of memory was potent with
Walter Scott. He loved the Past, he never
spoke of it but with admiration and respect,
he studied it, explored it, honored it ; not
the personal Past, which our egotism loves,
but the great Past of his countrymen. This
sentiment is the master quality in his novels, and gives them their peculiar interest.
There have been plenty of historical novels,
but none others bear those tender marks
of filial affection which characterize the Waverley Novels.

There is another quality in Scott closely
connected with his feeling for the Past,
which we in America, with our democratic
doctrines, find it more difficult to appreciate

justly. This quality, respect for rank, — a very inadequate and inexact phrase, — is part and parcel of a social condition very different from our own. Scott had an open, generous admiration for that diversity which gave free play to the virtues of loyalty and gratitude on one side, and of protection and solicitude on the other. The Scottish laird and his cotters had reciprocal duties; instead of crying "Each man for himself!" they enjoyed their mutual dependence. The tie of chieftain and clansman bore no great dissimilarity to that of father and son, new affections were called out, a gillie took pride in his chief, and the chief was fond of his gillie.

Scott's respect for rank was as far removed from snobbery as he from Hecuba; it was not only devoid of all meanness, but it had a childlike, a solemn, and admirable element, a kind of acceptance of society as established by the hand of God. Added to this solemn acceptance was his artistic pleasure in the picturesque variety and gradation of rank, as in a prospect where the ground rises from flatness, over undulating meadows, to rolling hills and ranges of mountains. It is exhilarating to behold even seeming greatness, and the perspective of rank throws into high relief persons of birth and office, and cunningly produces the effect of greatness. That patriotism which clings to flag or king, with Scott attached itself to the social order. He was intensely loyal to the structure of society in which he lived, not because he was happy and prosperous under it, but because to him it was noble and beautiful. When a project for innovations in the law courts was proposed, he was greatly moved. " No, no," said he to Jeffrey, " little by little, whatever your wishes may be, you will destroy and undermine, until nothing of what makes Scotland Scotland shall remain ; " and the tears gushed down his cheeks. The social system of clanship, " We Scots are a clannish body," made this sentiment easy ; he felt toward his chief and his clan as a veteran feels toward his colonel and his regiment.

To Scott's historic sentiment and tenderness of feeling for the established social order was added a love of place, begotten of associations with pleasant Teviotdale, the Tweed, Leader Haughs, the Braes of Yar-

row, bequeathed from generation to generation. We Americans, men of migratory
habits, who do not live where our fathers
have lived, or, if so, pull their houses down
that we may build others with modern luxury, are strangers to the deep sentiment
which a Scotsman cherishes for his home;
— not the mere stones and timber, which
keep him dry and warm, but the hearth at
which his mother and his forefathers sat and
took their ease after the labor of the day, the
ancient trees about the porch, the heather
and honeysuckle, the highroad down which
galloped the post with news of Waterloo and
Culloden, the little brooks of border min-
strelsy, and the mountains of legend ; we do
not share his inward feeling that his soul is
bound to the soul of the place by some rite
celebrated long before his birth, that for
better or worse they two are mated, and not
without some hidden injury can anything
but death part them.   Perhaps such feelings
are childish, they certainly are not modish
according to our American notions, but over
those who entertain them they are royally
tyrannical.   It was so with Scott, and though
when left to ourselves we may not feel that

feeling, he teaches us a lively sympathy with it, and gives us a deeper desire to have what we may really call a home.

Scott also possessed a great theatrical imagination. He looked on life as from an upper window, and watched the vast historical pageant march along; his eye caught notable persons, dramatic incidents, picturesque episodes, with the skill of a sagacious theatre manager. Not the drama of conscience, not the meetings and maladjustments of different temperaments and personalities, not the whims of an over-civilized psychology, not the sensitive indoor happenings of life : but scenes that startle the eye, alarm the ear, and keep every sense on the alert; the objective bustle and much ado of life; the striking effects which contrast clothes as well as character, bringing together Highlander and Lowlander, Crusader and Saracen, jesters, prelates, turnkeys, and foresters. That is why the Waverley Novels divide honors with the theatre in a boy's life. I can remember how easy seemed the transition from my thumbed and dog-eared " Guy Mannering " to the front row of the pit, which my impatience reached in ample time to study the curtain resplendent with Boccaccio's garden before it was lifted on a wonderful world of romance wherein the *jeune premier* stepped forward like Frank Osbaldistone, Sir Kenneth, or any of "my insipidly imbecile young men," as Scott called them, to play his difficult, ungrateful part, just as they did, with awkwardness and self-conscious inability, while the audience passed him by, as readers do in the Waverley Novels, to gaze on the glittering *mise en scène,* and watch the real heroes of the piece.

The melodramatic theatre indicates certain fundamental truths of human nature. We have inherited traits of the savage, we delight in crimson and sounding brass, in soldiers and gypsies, nor can we conceal, if we would, another and nearer ancestry, "The child is father to the man:" the laws of childhood govern us still, and it is to this common nature of Child and Man that Scott appeals so strongly.

> "Sound, sound the clarion, fill the fife!
> To all the sensual world proclaim,
> One crowded hour of glorious life
> Is worth an age without a name."

Scott was a master of the domain of simple

theatrical drama. What is there more effective than his bravado scenes, which we watch
with that secret sympathy for bragging with
which we used to watch the big boys at
school, for we know that the biggest words
will be seconded by deeds. " Touch Ralph
de Vipont's shield — touch the Hospitaller's
shield; he is your cheapest bargain." " 'Who
has dared,' said Richard, laying his hands
upon the Austrian standard, ' who has dared
to place this paltry rag beside the banner of
England?' " " ' Die, bloodthirsty dog!' said
Balfour, ' die as thou hast lived! die, like the
beasts that perish — hoping nothing — be-
lieving nothing ' — ' And fearing nothing ! '
said Bothwell." These, and a hundred such
passages, are very simple, but simple with a
simplicity not easy to attain ; they touch the
young barbarian in us to the quick.

In addition to these traits, Scott had that
shrewd practical understanding which is said
to mark the Scotsman. Some acute contemporary said that " Scott's sense was more
wonderful than his genius." In fact, his
sense is so all-pervasive that it often renders
the reader blind to the imaginative qualities
that spread their great wings throughout

most of the novels. It was this good sense
that enabled Scott to supply the admirable
framework of his stories, for it taught him
to understand the ways of men, — farmers,
shopkeepers, lawyers, soldiers, lairds, gra-
ziers, smugglers, — to perceive how all parts
of society are linked together, and to trace
the social nerves that connect the shepherd
and the blacksmith with historic personages.
Scott had great powers of observation, but
these powers, instead of being allowed to
yield at their own will to the temptation of
the moment, were always under the control
of good sense. This controlled observation,
aided by the extraordinary healthiness of his
nature, enabled him to look upon life with
so much largeness, and never suffered his
fancy to wander off and fasten on some sore
spot in the body social, or on some morbid
individual; but held it fixed on healthy society, on sanity and equilibrium. Natural,
healthy life always drew upon Scott's abundant sympathy. Dandie Dinmont, Mr. Old-
buck, Baillie Jarvie, and a hundred more
show the greatest pigment of art, the good
color of health. Open a novel almost at
random and you meet a sympathetic under-

standing. For example, a fisherwoman is
pleading for a dram of whiskey : " Ay, ay,
— it's easy for your honor, and like o' you
gentlefolks, to say sae, that hae stouth and
routh, and fire and fending, and meat and
claith, and sit dry and canny by the fireside.
But an' ye wanted fire and meat and dry
claise, and were deeing o' cauld, and had a
sair heart, whilk is warst ava', wi' just tip-
pence in your pouch, wadna ye be glad to
buy a dram wi' it, to be eilding and claise,
and a supper and heart's ease into the bargain till the morn's morning ? "

It is easy to disparage common sense and
the art of arousing boyish interest, just as it
is easy to disparage romantic affections for
the past, for rank, and for place ; but Scott
had a power which transfigured common
sense, theatrical imagination, and conserva-
tive sentiments, — Scott was a poet. His
poetic genius has given him one great advantage over all other English novelists. As
we think of the famous names, Fielding,
Richardson, Jane Austen, Thackeray, Dickens, Charlotte Brontë, George Eliot, Meredith ; according to our taste, our education,
or our whimsies, we prefer this quality in

one, we enjoy that in another, and we may,
as many do, put others above Scott in the
hierarchy of English novelists, but nobody,
not even the most intemperate, will compare
any one of them with Scott as a poet. Scott
had great lyrical gifts. It has been remarked
how many of his poems Mr. Palgrave has
inserted in the "Golden Treasury." Palgrave did well. There are few poems that
have the peculiar beauty of Scott's lyrics.
Take, for example, —

> " A weary lot is thine, fair maid,
>   A weary lot is thine!
> To pull the thorn thy brow to braid,
>   And press the rue for wine.
> A lightsome eye, a soldier's mien,
>   A feather of the blue,
> A doublet of the Lincoln green —
>   No more of me you knew,
>   My love!
> No more of me you knew."

What maiden could resist

> " A lightsome eye, a soldier's mien,
>   A feather of the blue ? "

Scott's poetic nature, delicate and charming as it is in his lyrics, picturesque and
vigorous as it is in his long poems, finds its
sturdier and most natural expression in his
novels; in them it refines the prodigal dis-

play of pictorial life, it bestows lightness and vividness, it gives an atmosphere of beauty, and a joyful exhilaration of enfranchisement from the commonplace; it mingles the leaven of poetry into ordinary life, and causes what we call romance. Take, for example, a subject like war. War, as it is, commissariat, dysentery, mule-trains, six-pounders, disemboweled boys, reconcentration, water-cure, lying, and swindling, has been described by Zola and Tolstoi with the skill of that genius which is faithful to the naked-ness of fact. But for the millions who do not go to the battlefield, hospital, or burial-ditch, war is another matter; for them it is a brilliant affair of colors, drums, uniforms, courage, enthusiasm, heroism, and victory; it is the most brilliant of stage-shows, the most exciting of games. This is the familiar conception of war; and Scott has expressed his thorough sympathy with immense poeti-cal skill. Let the sternest Quaker read the battle scene in " Marmion," and he will feel his temper glow with warlike ardor; and the fighting in the novels, for instance the battle in " Old Mortality," is still better. In like manner in the pictures of Highland life the

style may be poor, the workmanship careless,
but we are always aware that what we read
has been written by one who looked upon
what he describes with a poet's eye.

The poetry that animates the Waverley
Novels was not, as with some men, a rare
accomplishment kept for literary use, but lay
deep in Scott's life. As a young man he
fell in love with a lady who loved and married another, and all his life her memory,
etherealized no doubt after the manner of
poets and lovers, stayed with him, so that
despite the greatest worldly success his finer
happiness lay in imagination. But as he
appeared at Abbotsford, gayest among the
gay, prince of good fellows, what comrade
conjectured that the poet had not attained
his heart's desire?

III

It is easy to find fault with Scott; he has
taken no pains to hide the bounds of his
genius. He was careless to slovenliness, he
hardly ever corrected his pages, he worked
with a glad animal energy, writing two or
three hours before breakfast every morning, chiefly in order to free himself from the

pressure of his fancy. So lightly did he go
to work that when taken sick after writing
"The Bride of Lammermoor " he forgot all
but the outline of the plot. His pen coursed
like a greyhound ; at times it lost the scent
of the story and strayed away into tedious
prologue and peroration, or in endless talk,
and then, the scent regained, it dashed on
into a scene of unequaled vigor and imagination.   There are few speeches that can rank
with that of Jeanie Deans to Queen Caroline:
" But when the hour of trouble comes to the
mind or to the body — and seldom may it
visit your Leddyship — and when the hour
of death comes, that comes to high and low
— lang and late may it be yours — O my
Leddy, then it isna what we hae dune for
oursells, but what we hae dune for others,
that we think on maist pleasantly.   And the
thoughts that ye hae intervened to spare the
puir thing's life will be sweeter in that hour,
come when it may, than if a word of your
mouth could hang the haill Porteous mob at
the tail of ae tow."

Scott was a vigorous, happy man, who
rated life far higher than literature, and
looked upon novel-writing as a money-getting

operatibn. "'I'd rather be a kitten and cry
Mew,'" he said, "than write the best poetry
in the world on condition of laying aside
common sense in the ordinary transactions
and business of the world." He would have
entertained pity, not untouched by scorn, for
those novelists who apply to a novel the rules
that govern a lyric, and come home fatigued
from a day spent in seeking an adjective.
Scott wrote with what is called inspiration;
when he had written, his mind left his manuscript and turned to something new. No
doubt we wish that it had been otherwise,
that Scott, in addition to his imaginative
power, had also possessed the faculty of self-
criticism; perhaps Nature has adopted some
self-denying ordinance, that, where she is so
prodigal with her right hand, she will be
somewhat niggard with the left. We are
hard to please if we demand that she shall
add the delicate art of Stevenson to the virile
power of Walter Scott.

There is a second fault; archæologists
tell us that no man ever spoke like King
Richard, Ivanhoe, and Locksley. Scott, however, has erred in good company. Did Moses
and David speak as the Old Testament nar-

rates ? Did knights-errant ever utter such
words as Malory puts into the mouth of
Perceval ? Or did the real Antony have
the eloquence of Shakespeare ? Historical
and archæological mistakes are serious in
history and archæology, and shockingly dis-
figure examination papers, but in novels the
standards are different. Perhaps men learned
in demonology are put out of patience by
" Paradise Lost " and the " Inferno," and
scholars in fairy lore vex themselves over
Ariel and Titania ; but " Ivanhoe " is like a
picture, which at a few feet shows blotches
and daubs, but looked at from the proper
distance, shows the correct outline and the
true color. The raw conjunction of Saxon
and Norman, the story how the two great
stocks of Englishmen went housekeeping
together, is told better than in any history.
So it is with " The Talisman." The picture
of the crusading invasion of Palestine is no
doubt wholly incorrect in all details, and yet
what book equals it in enabling us to understand the romantic attitude of Europe and the
great popular Christian sentiment which expressed itself in unchristian means and built
so differently from what it knew ? But we

need not quarrel in defense of "Ivanhoe," or "Quentin Durward," or "The Talisman." Unquestionably the Scottish novels are the best, "Rob Roy," "Guy Mannering," "The Antiquary," "Old Mortality," "The Heart of Mid-Lothian;" in them we find portraiture of character, drawn with an art that must satisfy the most difficult advocate of studies from life; and probably all of Scott's famous characters were drawn from life.

A more serious charge is that Scott is not interested in the soul; that the higher domains of human faculties, love and religion, are treated not at all or else inadequately. At first sight there seems to be much justice in this complaint, for if our minds run over the names of the Waverley Novels, — the very titles, like a romantic tune, play a melody of youth, — we remember no love scene of power, nor any lovable woman except Diana Vernon, and the religion in them is too much like that which fills up our own Sunday mornings between the fishballs of breakfast and the cold roast beef of dinner. Carlyle has expressed his dissatisfaction with Scott's shortcomings, after the manner of an eloquent advocate who sets forth his case,

and leaves the jury to get at justice as best
they may. He denies that Scott touches the
spiritual or ethical side of life, and therefore
condemns him. But Carlyle does not look
for ethics except in exhortations, nor for
spiritual life except in a vociferous crying
after God; whereas the soul is wayward and
strays outside of metaphysics and of right-
eous indignation. That Scott himself was a
good man, in a very high and solemn significance of those words, cannot be questioned
by any one who has read his biography and
letters. No shadow of self-deception clouded
his mind when, in moments of great physical
pain, he said, "I should be a great fool,
and a most ungrateful wretch, to complain
of such inflictions as these. My life has
been in all its private and public relations as
fortunate, perhaps, as was ever lived, up to
this period; and whether pain or misfortune
may lie behind the dark curtain of futurity,
I am already a sufficient debtor to the bounty
of Providence to be resigned to it;" nor
when he thought he was dying, "For myself I am unconscious of ever having done
any man an injury or omitted any fair opportunity of doing any man a benefit." Every

one knows his last words, "Lockhart, be a
good man — be virtuous — be religious —
be a good man. Nothing else will give you
any comfort when you come to lie here."

Ethics have two methods: one is the way of
the great Hebrew prophets who cry, "Woe
to the children of this world! Repent, repent!" and Carlyle's figure, as he follows
their strait and narrow way, shows very
heroic on the skyline of life; but there is
still room for those teachers of ethics who
follow another method, who do not fix their
eyes on the anger of God, but on the beautiful world which He has created. To them
humanity is not vile, nor this earth a magnified Babylon; they look for virtue and they
find it; they see childhood ruddy-cheeked
and light-hearted, youth idealized by the
enchantment of first love; they rejoice in a
wonderful world; they laugh with those who
laugh, weep with mourners, dance with the
young, are crutches to the old, tell stories to
the moping, throw jests to the jolly, comfort
cold hearts, and leave everywhere a ripening
warmth like sunlight, and a faith that happiness is its own justification. This was the
way of Walter Scott.

No doubt spiritual life can express itself
in cries and prophecies, yet for most men,
looking over chequered lives, or into the re-
cesses of their own hearts, the spiritual life
is embodied not in loud exhortations and
threats, but rather in honor, loyalty, truth;
and those who let this belief appear in their
daily life are entitled to the name, toward
which they are greatly indifferent, of spiritual
teachers. Honor, loyalty, truth, were very
dear to Walter Scott; his love for them appears throughout his biography. He says,
" It is our duty to fight on, doing what good
we can and trusting to God Almighty, whose
grace ripens the seeds we commit to the
earth, that our benefactions shall bear fruit."
Among the good seeds Scott committed to
the earth are his novels, which, if they are
not spiritual, according to the significance
of that word as used by prophet and priest,
have that in them which has helped generations of young men to admire manliness,
purity, fair play, and honor, and has strengthened their inward resolutions to think no
unworthy thoughts, to do no unworthy
deeds. Literature, not preaching, has been
the great civilizer; if it has not been as

quick to kindle enthusiasm for large causes, it has acted with greater sureness and has built more permanently; and of all the great names in literature as a power for good, who shall come next to Shakespeare, Dante, and Cervantes, if not Walter Scott?

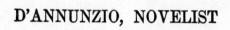

D'ANNUNZIO, NOVELIST

D'ANNUNZIO, NOVELIST

"'TOM JONES' and Gray's 'Elegy in a Country Churchyard' are both excellent, and much spoke of by both sex, particularly by the men." This statement by Marjorie Fleming has abundant confirmation in the history of English literature for the last hundred and fifty years. And although this nineteenth century of ours has enjoyed throwing a great many stones at the eighteenth, we must acknowledge that we cannot find in English literature another novel and another poem that, taken together, give us a fuller knowledge of English-speaking men. There are times, in the twilights of the day, and of the year, in the closing in of life, when we all contemplate death; and the Elegy tells all our thoughts in lines that possess our memories like our mothers' voices. It shows simple folk in sight of death, calm, natural, serious, high-minded. Thomas a Kempis, Cato the younger, the cavaliers of the Light Bri-

gade, may have thought upon death after
other fashions, but for most of us the
thoughts of our hearts have been portrayed
by Gray.

" Tom Jones " is the contemplation of life
in ordinary Englishmen. In the innocent days
before Mr. Hardy and some other writers of
distinction " Tom Jones " was reputed coarse,
— one of those classics that should find their
places on a shelf well out of reach of young
arms.   The manners of Squire Western and
of Tom himself are such as often are best
described in the Squire's own language. But
who is the man, as Thackeray says, that does
not feel freer after he has read the book?
Fielding, in his rough and ready way, has
described men as they are, made of the dust
of the earth, and that not carefully chosen.
We no longer read it aloud to our families,
as was the custom of our great-grandfathers;
but we do not all read Mr. Hardy aloud to
our daughters. "Tom Jones" is a big, strong,
fearless, honest book ; it gives us a hearty
slap on the back, congratulating us that we
are alive, and we accept the congratulation
with pleasure. Its richness is astonishing.
It has flowed down through English litera-

ture like a fertilizing Nile. In it we find
the beginnings of Sheridan, Dickens, Thackeray, George Eliot. In it we have those
wonderful conversations between Square and
Thwackum, which remind us of Don Quixote
and Sancho Panza. Mrs. Seagrim talks for
half a page, and we hold our noses against
the smells in her kitchen.

The power of the book is its eulogy upon
life. Is it not wretched to be stocks, stones,
tenants of Westminster Abbey, mathemati-
cians, or young gentlemen lost in philosophy? Is not the exhilaration of wine good?
Is not dinner worth the eating? Do not
young women make a most potent and
charming government? Fielding takes immense pleasure in the foolishness, in the foibles of men, and he finds amusement in their
vices, but over virtue and vice, over wisdom
and folly, he always insists upon the joy and
the value of life.

When we shall have re-read "Tom Jones"
and repeated Gray's Elegy to ourselves, then
we shall be in the mood in which we can
best determine the value of foreign novels
for us. And so, with this avowal of our
point of view, we approach the stories of the

distinguished Italian novelist, Gabriele d'Annunzio.

Men of action who apply themselves to literature are likely to have a generous confidence that skill will follow courage; that if they write, the capacity to write effectively will surely come. Plays, novels, editorials, sonnets, are written by them straight upon the impulse. They plunge into literature as if it were as buoyant as their spirit, and strike out like young sea creatures. Gabriele d'Annunzio is a man of another complexion. He is not a man of action, but of reflection. He is a student; he lives in the world of books. Through this many-colored medium of literature he sees men and women; but he is saved from an obvious artificiality by his sensitiveness to books of many kinds. He has submitted to laborious discipline; he has sat at the feet of many masters. His early schooling may be seen in a collection of stories published in 1886 under the name of the first, " San Pantaleone." One story is in imitation of Verga, another of de Maupassant ; and in " La Fattura " is an attempt to bring the humor of Boccaccio into a modern tale. Even in the "Decameron " this renowned humor has neither affection nor pity for father ; in its own cradle it mewls like an ill-mannered foundling. In the hands of d'Annunzio it acquires the ingenuous charm of Mr. Noah Claypole. We believe that d'Annunzio, consciously or unconsciously, became aware of his native antipathy to humor, for we have not found any other attempt at it in his work. It is in this absence of humor that we first feel the separation between d'Annunzio and the deep human feelings. In Italian literature there is no joyous, mellow, merry book, in which as a boy he might have nuzzled and rubbed off upon himself some fruitful pollen. One would as soon expect to find a portrait of Mr. Pickwick by Botticelli as the spirit of Dickens in any cranny of Italian literature. M. de Vogüé has said that d'Annunzio is born out of time ; that in spirit he is one of the *cinquecentisti*. There is something ferocious and bitter in him. The great human law of gravitation, that draws man to man, does not affect him.

Nevertheless, these stories have much vigor and skillful description. In " San Pantaleone " d'Annunzio depicts the frenzy and fierce emotions of superstition in southern Italy. Savage fanaticism interests him. The combination of high imagination and the exaltation of delirium with the stupidity and ignorance of beasts has a powerful attraction for him. The union of the intellectual and the bestial is to him the most remarkable phenomenon of life.

This early book is interesting also in that it shows ideas in the germ and in their first growth which are subsequently developed in the novels, and in that it betrays d'Annunzio's notion that impersonality — that deliverance from the frailty of humanity to which he would aspire — is an escape from compassion and affection, and is most readily come at through contempt.

D'Annunzio has spared no pains to make his language as melodious and efficient an instrument as he can. Italian prose has never been in the same rank with Italian poetry. There have been no great Italians whose genius has forced Italian prose to bear the stamp and impress of their personalities. In the sixteenth century this prose was clear and capable, but since then it has gradually shrunk to fit the thoughts of lesser men.

D'Annunzio has taken on his back the task
of liberating the Italian tongue; he will give
it " virtue, manners, freedom, power." Not
having within him the necessity of utterance,
not hurried on by impetuous talents, he has
applied himself to his task with deliberation
and circumspection. He has studied Boccaccio and Petrarch and many men of old,
so that his vocabulary shall be full, and his
grammar as pure and flexible as the genius
of the language will permit. He purposes
to fetch from their hiding-places Italian
words long unused, that he shall be at no
loss for means to make plain the most delicate distinctions of meaning. He intends
that his thoughts, which shall be gathered
from all intellectual Europe, shall have fit
words to house them.

At the time of his first novels, d'Annunzio turned to Paris, the capital of the Latin
world, as to his natural school. In Paris
men of letters (let us except a number of
gallant young gentlemen disdainful of readers) begin by copying and imitation, that
they may acquire the mechanical parts of
their craft. They study Stendhal, Flaubert,
de Maupassant; they contemplate a chapter,

they brood over a soliloquy, they grow lean over a dialogue. They learn how the master marshals his ideas, how he winds up to his climax, what tricks and devices he employs to take his reader prisoner. From time to time voices protestant are raised, crying out against the sacrifice of innocent originality. But the band of the lettered marches on. Why should they forego knowledge gathered together with great pains? Shall a young man turn against the dictionary?

In Paris d'Annunzio found a number of well-established methods for writing a novel. Some of these methods have had a powerful influence upon him; therefore it may be worth while to remind ourselves of them, in order that we may the better judge his capacity for original work and for faithful imitation.

The first method is simply that of the old-fashioned novel of character and manners, and needs no description.

The second method, the familiar philo-real or philo-natural, hardly may be said to be a method for writing a novel; it is a mode of writing what you will; but it has achieved its reputation in the hands of novelists. This

method is supposed to require careful, pains-
taking, and accurate observation of real persons, places, and incidents ; but in truth it
lets this duty sit very lightly on its shoulders, and commonly consists in descriptions,
minute, elaborate, prolix. It pretends to be
an apotheosis of fact ; it is a verbal ritual.
It has been used by many a man unconscious of schools. In practice it is the most
efficacious means of causing the illusion of
reality within the reach of common men.
By half a dozen pages of deliberate and exact enumeration of outward parts, a man
may frequently produce as vivid and memory-
haunting a picture as a poet does with a met-
aphor or an epithet. M. Zola, by virtue of
his vigor, his zeal, and his fecundity, has won
popular renown as leader of this school.

The third method is the psychological.
It consists in the delineation in detail of
thoughts and feelings instead of actions, the
inward and unseen in place of the outward
and visible. The novelist professes an intimate knowledge of the wheels, cogs, cranks
of the brain, and of the airy portraiture of
the mind, and he describes them with an
embellishment of scientific phrase, letting the

outward acts take care of themselves as best
they may. The danger of this method is
lest the portrayal of psychic states constitute
the novel, and lest the plot and the poor
little incidents squeeze in with much dis-
comfort. Perhaps M. Bourget is the most
distinguished member of this school.

The fourth mode is that of the *Symbolistes*.
These writers are not wholly purged from
all desire for self-assertion; they wish room
wherein openly to display themselves, and to
this end they have withdrawn apart out of
the shadow of famous names. They assert
that they stand for freedom from old saws;
that the philosophic doctrine of idealism up-
sets all theories based upon the reality of
matter; that the business of art is to use the
imperfect means of expression at its command to suggest and indicate ideas; that
character, action, incidents, are but symbols
of ideas. They hold individuality sacred,
and define it to be that which man has in
himself unshared by any other, and deny the
name to all that he has in common with
other men. Therefore this individuality,
being but a small part, a paring, as it were,
of an individual, shows maimed and unnat-

ural. And thus they run foul of seeming opposites, both the individual and also the abstract; for the revered symbol is neither more nor less than an essence abstracted from the motley company of individuals, filtered and refined, which returns decked out in the haberdashery of generalities, under the baptismal name of symbol. In order to facilitate this latter process of extracting and detaching unity from multiplicity, they murmur songs of mystic sensuality, as spiritualists burn tapers of frankincense at the disentanglement of a spirit from its fellows in the upper or nether world. One of the best known of these is Maurice Maeterlinck.

There is, moreover, a doctrine that runs across these various methods, like one pattern across cloths of divers materials, which affects them all. It is that the writer shall persistently obtrude himself upon the reader. Stated in this blunt fashion, the doctrine is considered indecent; it is not acknowledged; and, in truth, these Frenchmen do not reveal their personality. It may indeed be doubted if they have any such encumbrance. In its place they have a bunch of theories tied up with the ribbon of their literary experience;

and the exhalations of it, as if it were a bunch of flowers, they suffer to transpire through their pages. These theories are not of the writer's own making; they are the notions made popular in Paris by a number of distinguished men, of whom the most notable are Taine and Renan. The inevitable sequence of cause and effect and its attendant corollaries, vigorously asserted and reiterated by M. Taine, and the amiable irony of M. Renan, have had success with men of letters out of all proportion to their intellectual value. Their theories have influenced novels very much, and life very little. Why should the dogmas of determinism and of unskeptical skepticism affect men in a novel more obviously than they affect men in the street?

Into this world of Parisian letters, in among these literary methods, walked young d'Annunzio, sensitive, ambitious, detached from tradition, with his ten talents wrapped up in an embroidered and scented napkin, with his docile apprentice habit of mind, and straightway set himself, with passion for art and the ardor of youth, to the task of acquiring these French methods, that he should

become the absolute master of his talents,
and be able to put them out at the highest
rate of usury. Young enough to be seduced
by the blandishments of novelty, he passed
over the old-fashioned way of describing
character, and studied the methods of the
realists, the psychologists, the symbolists.
With his clear, cool head he very soon mas-
tered their methods, and in the achievement
quickened and strengthened his artistic capacities, his precision, his sense of proportion,
his understanding of form. But the nurture
of his art magnified and strengthened his
lack of humanity. Lack of human sympathy
is a common characteristic of young men
who are rich in enthusiasm for the written
word, the delineated line, the carving upon
the cornice. Devotion to the minute refine-
ments of art seems to leave no room in their
hearts for human kindliness. The unripe-
ness of youth, overwork, disgust with the
common in human beings, help to separate
them from their kind. In their weariness
they forget that the great masters of art are
passionately human. D'Annunzio does not
wholly admit that he is a human unit, and
his sentiment in this matter has made him

all the more susceptible to literary influences. We find in him deep impressions from his French studies. He has levied tribute upon Zola, Bourget, and Loti.

In 1889 d'Annunzio published " Il Piacere." He lacks, as we have said, strong human feelings; he does not know the interest in life as life ; he has no zeal to live, and from the scantiness and barrenness of his external world he turns to the inner world of self. M. de Vogüé has pointed out that his heroes, Sperelli, Tullio Hermil, and Georgio Aurispa, are all studies of himself. D'Annunzio does not deny this. He would argue that it would be nonsense to portray others, as we know ourselves best. Sperelli, the hero of " Il Piacere," is an exact portrait of himself. He is described as " the perfect type of a young Italian gentleman in the nineteenth century, the true representative of a stock of gentlemen and dainty artists, the last descendant of an intellectual race. He is saturated with art. His wonderful boyhood has been nourished upon divers profound studies. From his father he acquired a taste for artistic things, a passionate worship of beauty, a paradoxical disdain for prejudice, avidity for pleasure. His education was a living thing; it was not got out of books, but in the glare of human reality." The result was that " Sperelli chose, in the practice of the arts, those instruments that are difficult, exact, perfect, that cannot be put to base uses, — versification and engraving ; and he purposed strictly to follow and to renew the forms of Italian tradition, binding himself with fresh ties to the poets of the *new style* and to the painters who came before the Renaissance. His spirit was formal in its very essence. He valued expression more than thought. His literary essays were feats of dexterity; studies devoted to research, technique, the curious. He believed with Taine that it would be more difficult to write six beautiful lines of poetry than to win a battle. His story of an hermaphrodite was imitative, in its structure, of the story of ' Orpheus ' by Poliziano ; it had verses of exquisite delicacy, melody, and force, especially in the choruses sung by monsters of double form, — centaurs, sirens, sphinxes. His tragedy ' La Simona,' composed in lyrical metre, was of a most curious savor. Although its rhymes obeyed the old Tuscan models, it seemed as if it had been begotten in the fancy of an Elizabethan poet by a story from the ' Decameron ; ' it held something of that music, rich and strange, which is in some of Shakespeare's minor plays."

" Il Piacere " is a study of the passion of love. Sperelli's love for Elena, and afterwards for Maria, is made the subject of an essay in the guise of a novel upon two aspects of this passion. The first is the union of mind, almost non-human, unacquainted with life as if new-born, with the fact of sex. D'Annunzio takes this fact of sex in its simplest form, and portrays its effects upon the mind in the latter's most sequestered state, separate and apart, uninfluenced by human things, divorced from all humanity. He observes the isolated mind under the dominion of this fact, and describes it in like manner as he depicts the sea blown upon by the wind. The shifting push of emotion, the coming and going of thought, the involutions and intricacy of momentary feeling, the whirl of fantastic dreams, the swoop and dash of memory, the grasp at the absolute, the rocket-like whir of the imagination, — all the motions of the mind, like the surface of a stormy sea, toss and froth before you.

Sperelli's love for Maria, at least in the beginning, is as lovely as a girl could wish. It may be too much akin to his passion for art, it may have in it too much of the ichor that flowed in Shelley's veins. It is delicate, ethereal; it is the passion of a dream man for a dream maiden. It feeds on beauty; yet "like a worm i' the bud." "But long it could not be, till that" his baser nature "pull'd the poor wretch from its melodious lay to muddy death." Yet the book is full of poetry. We hardly remember chapters in any novel that can match in charm those that succeed the narrative of the duel. We must free ourselves from habit by an effort, and put out of our simple *bourgeois* minds the fact that Maria has made marriage vows to another man; and we are able to do this, for the husband has no claims upon her except from those vows, and the poetry of the episode ends long before those vows are broken.

This novel, like the others, is decorated, enameled, and lacquered with cultivation. They are all like Christmas trees laden with alien fruit, — tinsel, candles, confectionery, anything that will catch the eye. England, France, Germany, Russia, contribute. Painting, sculpture, architecture, music, poetry, are called upon to give color, form, structure, sound, and dreaminess to embellish the descriptions. The twelfth, thirteenth, fourteenth, fifteenth, eighteenth, and nineteenth centuries parade before us in long pageant, — " L'uno e l'altro Guido," Gallucci, Memling, Bernini, Pollajuolo, Pinturicchio, Storace, Watteau, Shelley, Rameau, Bach, Gabriel Rossetti, Bizet. The charm of a woman for him is that she resembles a Madonna by Ghirlandajo, an intaglio by Niccolò Niccoli, a quatrain by Cino. His ladies are tattooed with resemblances, suggestions, proportions, similarities. The descriptions of their attractions read like an index to " The Stones of Venice." He does not disdain to translate Shelley's verse into Italian prose without quotation marks. This passion for art is d'Annunzio's means of escaping the vulgarity of common men ; it is his refuge, his cleft in the rock, whither he may betake himself, and in which he may enjoy the pleasures of intellectual content and scorn. This taste emphasizes his lack of human kindliness, and it heightens the effect of unreality; moreover it limits and clips off the interest of the common reader. D'Annunzio is like Mr. Pater in his nice tastes. He has noticed that the sentences of men who write from a desire to go hand in hand with other men, from an eagerness to propagate their own beliefs, trudge and plod, swinging their clauses and parentheses like loosely strapped panniers; that they observe regulations that should be broken, and break rules that should be kept. Therefore he girds himself like a gymnast, and with dainty mincing periods glides harmonious down the page; but his grace sometimes sinks into foppishness. He would defend himself like Lord Foppington in the play.

"*Tom.* Brother, you are the prince of coxcombs.

"*Lord Foppington.* I am *praud* to be at the head of so prevailing a party."

But even d'Annunzio's great skill cannot rescue him from obvious artificiality. He lives in a hothouse atmosphere of abnormal refinement, at a temperature where only creatures nurtured to a particular degree and a

half Fahrenheit can survive. Sometimes one
is tempted to believe that d'Annunzio, conscious of his own inhumanity, deals with the
passions in the vain hope to lay hand upon
the human. He hovers like a non-human
creature about humanity, he is eager to
know it, he longs to become a man ; and
Setebos, his god, at his supplication turns
him into a new form. The changeling thinks
he is become a man ; but lo ! he is only an
intellectual beast.

Our judgment of d'Annunzio's work, however, is based upon other considerations than
that of the appropriate subordination of his
cultivation to his story. It depends upon our
theory of human conduct and our philosophy
of life, upon our answers to these questions :
Has the long, long struggle to obtain new
interests — interests that seem higher and
nobler than the old, interests the record of
which constitutes the history of civilization
—been mere unsuccessful folly? Are the
chief interests in life the primary instincts?
Are we no richer than the animals, after all
these toiling years of renunciation and self-
denial? Is the heritage which we share with
the beasts the best that our fathers have

handed down to us? There seem to be in some corners of our world persons who answer these questions in the affirmative, saying, "Let us drop hypocrisy, let us face facts and know ourselves, let English literature put off false traditions and deal with the realities of life," and much more, all sparkling with brave words. Persons like Mr. George Moore, who have a profound respect for adjectives, say these instincts are *primary*, they are *fundamental*, and think that these two words, like "open sesame," have admitted us into the cave of reality. We are unable to succumb to the hallucination. The circulation of the blood is eminently primary and fundamental, yet there was literature of good repute before it was dreamed of. For ourselves, we find the interests of life in the secondary instincts, in the thoughts, hopes, sentiments, which man has won through centuries of toil, — here a little, there a little. We find the earlier instincts interesting only as they furnish a struggle for qualities later born. We are bored and disgusted by dragons of the prime until we hear the hoofs of St. George's horse and see St. George's helmet glitter in the sun. The dragon is no more

interesting than a cockroach, except to prove
the prowess of the hero. The bucking horse
may kick and curvet; we care not, till the
cowboy mount him. These poor primary
instincts are mere bulls for the toreador,
wild boars for the chase; they are our measures for strength, self-denial, fortitude, courage, temperance, chastity. The instinct of
self-preservation is the ladder up which the
soldier, the fireman, the lighthouse-keeper,
lightly trip to fame. What is the primary
and fundamental fear of death? With whom
is it the most powerful emotion? " O my
son Absalom, my son, my son Absalom!
would God I had died for thee!" Is it with
mothers? Ask them.

D'Annunzio, with his predilections for aristocracy, thinks that these primary instincts
are of unequaled importance and interest
because of their long descent. He forgets
that during the last few thousand years
power has been changing hands; that democracy has come upon us; and that a virtue is judged by its value to-day, and not by
that which it had in the misty past. Literature is one long story of the vain struggles
of the primary instincts against the moral

nature of man. From "Œdipus Tyrannus"
to "The Scarlet Letter" the primary passions
are defeated and overcome by duty, religion,
and the moral law. The misery of broken law
outlives passion and tramples on its embers.
The love of Paolo and Francesca is swallowed
up in their sin. It is the like in Faust.
Earthly passion cannot avail against the
moral powers. This network of the imagination binds a man more strongly than iron
shackles. The relations of our souls, of our
higher selves, to these instincts, are what
absorb us. We are thrilled by the stories in
which moral laws, children of instinct, have
arisen and vanquished their fathers, as the
beautiful young gods overcame the Titans.
If duty loses its savor, life no longer is
salted. The primary passions may continue
to hurl beasts at one another; human interest
is gone. Were it not for conscience, honor,
loyalty, the primary instincts would never be
the subject of a story. They would stay in
the paddocks of physiological textbooks.

"What a piece of work is man" that he
has been able to cover a fact of animal life
with poetry more beautifully than Shakespeare dresses a tale from Bandello! He

has created his honor as wonderful as his love; soldiers, like so many poets, have digged out of cruelty and slaughter this jewel of life. Where is the instinct of self-preservation here? At Roncesvaux, when Charlemagne's rear-guard is attacked by overwhelming numbers, Roland denies Oliver's request that he blow his horn for help. His one thought is that poets shall not sing songs to his dishonor : —

"Male cançun n'en deit estre cantée."

And is the belief in chastity, which has run round the world from east to west, nothing but a superstition born of fear? Has it lasted so long only to be proved at the end a coward and a dupe? Is this sacrifice of self mere instinctive folly in the individual? Does he gain nothing by it? Are the worship of the Virgin Mary, the praise of Galahad, the joys of self-denial, no more than monkish ignorance and timidity?

We are of the opinion that *l'art de la pourriture* is popular because it is easily acquired. It deals with the crude, the simple, the undeveloped. It has little to do with the complicated, intertwined mass of re-

lations that binds the individual to all other
individuals whether he will or not.   It does
not try to unravel the conglomerate sum of
human ties.   It does not see the myriad influences that rain down upon a man from all
that was before him, from all that is contem-
poraneous with him; it does not know the
height above him, the depth beneath, the
mysteries of substance and of void.   It deals
with materials that offer no resistance, no
difficulty, and cannot take the noble and
enduring forms of persisting things.   It
ignores the great labors of the human mind,
and the transforming effect of them upon its
human habitation.   This art cannot give
immortality.   One by one the artists who
produce it drop off the tree of living literature and are forgotten.   The supreme passion
of love has been told by Dante : —

"Quel giorno più non vi leggemmo avante."

Does d'Annunzio think that he would have
bettered the passage?   In the great delineation of passion, vulgarity and indecency,
insults to manners, the monotony of vice,
are obliterated; the brutality of detail slinks
off in silence.

In 1892 d'Annunzio published "L'Innocente." In this novel, as M. de Vogüé has
pointed out, he has directed his powers of
imitation towards the great Russian novelists.
But his spirit and talents are of such different sort from those of Tourgenieff, Tolstoi,
and Dostoiewsky that the copy is of the outside and show. D'Annunzio's faculties have
not been able to incorporate and to assimi-
late anything of the real Slav; they are the
same, and express themselves in the same
way, in "L'Innocente" as in "Il Piacere."
We therefore pass to his most celebrated
novel, "Il Trionfo della Morte," published in
1894. A translation of it — that is, of as
much of it as was meet for French readers
—was soon after published in the "Revue
des Deux Mondes." This novel won the
approval of M. de Vogüé, and has made Gabriele d'Annunzio a famous name throughout Europe.

The plot, if we may use an old-fashioned
word to express new matter, is this : Georgio
Aurispa, a young man of fortune, who leads
a life of emptiness in Rome, one day meets
Ippolita, the wife of another man. On this
important day he has gone to hear Bach's

Passion Music in a private chapel, and there he sees the beautiful Ippolita. Bored and disgusted by coarse pleasures, he throws himself with rapture into a poetical passion for this pale-faced, charming, slender Roman woman. The story begins just before the second anniversary of their meeting in the chapel. The husband has absconded, and Ippolita lives with her family. No suggestion of a possible marriage is made, although Aurispa frequently meditates with anguish on the thought that she may forsake him. He is wholly given to examining his mind and feelings ; he follows their changes, he explains their causes, he anticipates their mutations. He picks up each sentiment delicately, like a man playing jackstraws, holds it suspended, contemplates it from this side and from that, balances it before the faceted mirror of his imagination, and then falls into a melancholy. He dandles his sentiment for her, he purrs over it, he sings to it snatches of psychical old tunes, he ministers to it, fosters it, cherishes it, weeps over it, wonders if it be growing or decreasing.

For some reasons of duty Ippolita is obliged to be away from Rome from time to time,

once in Milan with her sister. Aurispa hears
of her, that she is well, that she is gay. "*She
laughs!* Then she can laugh, away from
me; she can be gay! All her letters are full
of sorrow, of lamentation, of hopeless long-
ing." The English reader is taken back to
that scene in "The Rivals" where Bob
Acres tells Faulkland that he has met Miss
Melville in Devonshire, and that she is very
well.

"*Acres.* She has been the belle and spirit
of the company wherever she has been, — so
lively and entertaining! So full of wit and
humor!

"*Faulkland.* There, Jack, there. Oh,
by my soul! there is an innate levity in
woman that nothing can overcome. What!
happy, and I away!"

Aurispa is peculiarly sensitive; the bunches
of nerve fibres at the base of his brain, the
ganglia in his medulla oblongata, are ex-
traordinarily alert, delicate, and powerful.
Every sensation runs through them like a
galloping horse; memory echoes the beating of its hoofs, and imagination speeds it
on into the future, till it multiplies, expands,
and swells into a troop. Aurispa yearns to

lose himself in happiness, and then droops
despondent, for a sudden jog of memory reminds him that he was in more of an ecstasy
when he first met Ippolita than he is to-day.
"Where are those delicate sensations which
once I had? Where are those exquisite and
manifold pricks of melancholy, those deep
and twisted pains, wherein I lost my soul as
in an endless labyrinth?"

In the zeal of his desire for fuller, more
enduring pleasure, he takes Ippolita to a
lonely house beside the sea that shall be
their hermitage.

Aurispa feels that there are two conditions
necessary to perfect happiness: one that he
should be the absolute master of Ippolita,
the other that he should have unlimited independence himself. "There is upon earth
but one enduring intoxication: absolute certainty in the ownership of another, — certainty fixed and unshakable." Aurispa pro-
poses to attain this condition. He puts his
intelligence to slavish service in discovery
of a method by which he shall win that
larger life and perfect content of which almost all men have had visions and dreams.
Long ago Buddha sought and thought to

attain this condition. Long ago the Stoics
devised plans to loose themselves from the
knots that tie men to the common life of all.
Long ago the Christians meditated a philosophy that should free them from the bonds
of the flesh, that they might live in the
spirit. Heedless of their experience, Aurispa
endeavors to find his content in sensuality;
but once in their hermitage, he soon perceives
that the new life he sought is impossible.
He feels his love for Ippolita dwindle and
grow thin. He must physic it quickly or it
will die; and if love fail, nothing is left but
death. Sometimes he thinks of her as dead.
Once dead, she will become such stuff as
thoughts are made of, a part of pure idealism.
" Out from a halting and lame existence she
will pass into a complete and perfect life,
forsaking forever her frail and sinful body.
To destroy in order to possess, — there is no
other way for him who seeks the absolute in
love."

That was for Aurispa a continuing thought,
but first his fancy turned for help to the religious sensuousness of his race. " He had
the gift of contemplation, interest in symbol
and in allegory, the power of abstraction, an

extreme sensitiveness to suggestions by sight
or by word, an organic tendency to haunting
visions and to hallucinations." He lacked
but faith. At that time, superstition like a
wind swept over the southern part of Italy;
there were rumors of a new Messiah; an
emotional fever infected the whole country
round. A day's journey from the hermitage
lay the sanctuary of Casalbordino. Once the
Virgin had appeared there to a devout old
man, and had granted his prayer, and to
commemorate this miracle the sanctuary had
been built; and now the country-folk swarmed
to the holy place. Georgio and Ippolita go
thither. All the description of this place, as
a note tells us, is the result of patient observation. About the sanctuary are gathered
together men and women from far and near,
all in a state of high exaltation. Troop upon
troop singing, —

"Viva Maria!
Maria Evviva!"

trudge over the dusty roads. These people
d'Annunzio depicts with the quick eye and
the patient care of an Agassiz. Monstrous
heads, deformed chests, shrunken legs, club-
feet, distorted hands, swollen tumors, sores

of many colors, all loathsome diseases to
which flesh is heir and for which d'Annunzio's medical dictionary has names, are here
set forth. "How much morbid pathology
has done for the novelist!" he is reported to
have said. Certainly its value to d'Annunzio cannot be rated too high. Aurispa and
Ippolita, excited by the fanatic exaltation,
fight their way into the church. There a
miserable mass of huddled humanity, shriek-
ing for grace, struggles toward the altar rail.
Behind the rail, the fat, stolid-faced priests
gather up the offerings. The air is filled
with nauseous smells. The church is a hide-
ous charnel-house, roofing in physical disease
and mental deformity. Outside, mountebanks,
jugglers, gamesters, foul men and women,
intercept what part of the offerings they can.
The memory of this day made Aurispa and
Ippolita sick, — her for human pity, him for
himself; for he became conscious that there
is no power which can enthrall absolute pleasure. He had turned toward heaven to save
his life, and he has proved by experience his
belief in the emptiness of its grace.

With instinctive repulsion from death, he
looks for escape to thought. Thought which

has enslaved him may set him free. He
ponders upon the teaching of Nietzsche.
Away with the creeds of weakness, the evan-
gel of impotence! Assert the justice of injustice, the righteousness of power, the joy of
creation and of destruction! But Aurispa
cannot. Nothing is left him but death. He
abandons all wish for perfect union with
Ippolita, yet jealousy will not suffer him to
leave her alive. His love for her has turned
into hate. In his thoughts it is she that
hounds him to death like a personal demon.
He grows supersensitive. He cannot bear
the red color of underdone beef. He is
ready to die of a joint, in juicy pain. He
gathers together in a heap and gloats over
all that he finds disagreeable and repellent
in Ippolita. What was she but his creation?
"Now, as always, she has done nothing but
submit to the form and impressions that I
have made. Her inner life has always been
a fiction. When the influence of my suggestion is interrupted, she returns to her
own nature, she becomes a woman again, the
instrument of base passion. Nothing can
change her, nothing can purify her." And
at last, by treachery and force, he drags her

with him over a precipice to death beneath.

Such is the plot, but there is no pretense that the plot is interesting or important except as a scaffold on which to exhibit a philosophy of life. That philosophy is clearly the author's philosophy. D'Annunzio's novel shows in clear view and distinct outline how the whirligig of time brings about its revenges.

Bishop Berkeley made famous the simple theory of idealism,— that a man cannot go outside of the inclosure of his mind; that the material world is the handiwork of fancy, with no reality, no length, nor breadth, nor fixedness; that the pageant of life is the march of dreams. Berkeley expected this theory to destroy materialism, skepticism, and infidelity. It did, in argument. Many a man has taken courage in this unanswerable retort to the materialist. He slings this theory, like a smooth pebble from the brook, at the Goliaths who advance with the ponderous weapons of scientific discovery.

The common idealist keeps his philosophy for his library, and walks abroad like his neighbors, subject to the rules, beliefs, and habits of common sense. But d'Annunzio,

who has received and adopted a bastard scion
of this idealism, is, as befits a man of leisure
and of letters, more faithful to his philosophy.
He has set forth his version of the theory in
this novel with characteristic clearness. Aurispa looks on the world as an instrument
that shall serve his pleasure. He will play
upon it what tunes he can that he may enjoy
the emotions and passions of life. He is
separate from his family and has a private
fortune. His world is small and dependent
upon him. In this world Aurispa has no
rival; in it there is no male thing to bid him
struggle for supremacy; it is his private property, and the right of private property is
fixed as firm beyond the reach of question as
the fact of personal existence. Gradually a
transformation takes place; this well-ordered
and obedient world changes under the dominion of Aurispa's thought. Little by little
object and subject lose their identity; like
the thieves of the Seventh Bolge in the Inferno, they combine, unite, form but one
whole. In this change the material world is
swallowed up, and out from the transformation crawls the ideal world of Aurispa's
thought : —

" Ogni primaio aspetto ivi era casso ;
Due e nessun l' imagine perversa
Parea, e tal sen gía con lento passo."

This ideal world is Aurispa's. It varies with
his volition, for it is the aggregate of his
thoughts, and they are the emanations of his
will. In this dominion he stands like a de-
generate Cæsar, drunk with power, frenzied
with his own potent impotence. Everything
is under his control, and yet there is a something imperceptible, like an invisible wall,
that bars his way to perfect pleasure. He
wanders all along it, touching, feeling, grop-
ing, all in vain. Think subtly as he will, he
finds no breach. Yet his deepest, his only
desire is to pass beyond. Perhaps life is this
barrier. He will break it down, and find his
absolute pleasure in death. And in exasper-
ation of despair before this invisible obstacle
he has recourse to action. In the presence
of action his ideal world wrestles once more
with reality, and amid the struggles Aurispa
finds that the only remedy for his impotent
individuality is to die. Both idealism and
fact push him towards death.

If we choose to regard Aurispa as living
in a real world, as a man responsible for his

acts, as a member of human society, we have little to say concerning him. He is a timid prig, a voluptuous murderer, an intellectual fop, smeared with self-love, vulgar to the utmost refinement of vulgarity, cruel, morbid, a flatterer, and a liar.

For poor Ippolita we have compassion. Had she lived out of Aurispa's world, with her alluring Italian nature she might have been charming. There is a rare feminine attractiveness about her : had she been subject to sweet influences, had she been born to Tourgenieff, she would have been one of the delightful women of fiction. All that she does has an attendant possibility of grace, eager to become incorporate in action. Delicacy, sensitiveness, affection, fitness for the gravity and the gayety of life, hover like ministering spirits just beyond the covers of the book ; they would come down to her, but they cannot. This possibility died before its birth. Ippolita's unborn soul, like the romantic episode in "Il Piacere," makes us feel that d'Annunzio may hereafter break loose from his theories, free himself from his cigarette-smoking philosophy, smash the looking-glass in front of which he sits copying his

own likeness, and start anew, able to understand the pleasures of life and prepared to
share in the joys of the struggle.   Surely M.
de Vogüé is looking at these indications of
creative ability and poetic thought, and not
at accomplishment, when he hails d'Annunzio
as the leader of another Italian Renaissance.
It is hope that calls forth M. de Vogüé's
praise.   A national literature has never yet
been built upon imitation, sensuality, and
artistic frippery.

After finishing the last page of " The Triumph of Death," quick as a flash we pass
through many phases of emotion. In the instant of time before the book leaves our hand,
our teeth set, our muscles contract, we desire
to hit out from the shoulder.   Our memory
teems with long-forgotten physical acts, up-
per-cuts, left-handers, swingers, knock-outs.
By some mysterious process, words that our
waking mind could not recall surge up in
capital letters ; all the vocabulary of Shake-
spearean insult rings in our ears, — base,
proud, shallow, beggarly, silk-stocking knave,
a glass-gazing finical rogue, a coward, a
pander, a cullionly barber-monger, a smooth-
tongued bolting-hutch of beastliness.   Our

thoughts bound like wild things from prize-
fights to inquisitors, from them to Iroquois,
to devils. Then succeeds the feeling as of
stepping on a snake, a sentiment as of a
struggle between species of animals, of instinctive combat for supremacy; no sense of
ultimate ends or motives, but the sudden
knowledge that our gorge is rising and that
we will not permit certain things. We raise
no question of reason; we put aside intelligence, and say, The time is come for life
to choose between you and us. The book,
after leaving our hand, strikes the opposite
wall and flutters to the floor. We grow
calmer; we draw up an indictment; we will
try Aurispa-d'Annunzio before a jury of
English-speaking men. Call the tale. Colonel Newcome! Adam Bede! Baillie Jarvie!
Tom Brown! Sam Weller! But nonsense!
these men are not eligible. Aurispa-d'Annunzio must be tried by a jury of his peers.
By this time we have recovered our compo-
sure, and rejoice in the common things of
life, — shaving-brushes, buttoned boots, cra-
vats, counting-stools, vouchers, ledgers, newspapers. All the multitude of little things,
forgiving our old discourtesy, heap coals of

fire upon our heads with their glad proofs
of reality. For a moment we can draw aside
" the veil of familiarity " from common life
and behold the poetry there; we bless our
simple affections and our daily bread. The
dear kind solid earth stands faithful and
familiar under our feet. How beautiful it
is!

> " Die unbegreiflich hohen Werke
> Sind herrlich wie am ersten Tag."

D'Annunzio's latest novel, " Le Vergini
delle Rocce," was published in 1896. In it
he appears as a symbolist, and by far the
most accomplished of the school. The story
is not of real people, but concerns the inhabitants of some spiritual world, as if certain instantaneous ideas of men, divorced
from the ideas of the instant before and of
the instant after, and therefore of a weird,
unnatural look, had been caught there and
kept to inhabit it, and should thenceforward
live after their own spiritual order, with no
further relations to humanity. These figures bear no doubtful resemblance to the
men and women in the pictures of Dante
Rossetti and of Burne-Jones. One might
fancy that a solitary maid gazing into a

beryl stone would see three such strangely beautiful virgins, Massimilla, Anatolia, Violante, move their weary young limbs daintily in the crystal sphere.

The landscape is the background of an English preraphaelite painter. Here d'Annunzio's style is in its delicate perfection. It carries these three strange and beautiful ladies along, as the river that runs down to many - towered Camelot bore onward the shallop of the Lady of Shalott. It is translucent; everything mirrors in it with a delicate sensitiveness, as if it were the mind of some fairy asleep, in which nothing except what is lovely and harmonious could reflect, and as if the slightest discord, the least petty failure of grace, would wake the sleeper and end the images forever. D'Annunzio's sentences have the quality of an incantation. This is the work of a master apprentice. But there the mastery ends. A story so far removed from life, a fairy story, must have order and law of its own, must be true to itself; or else it must move in some fairy plane parallel to human life, and never pretermit its correspondence with humanity.

Claudio, the teller of the story, is a scion

of a noble Italian family, of which one Alessandro had been the most illustrious member.
When the tale begins Claudio is riding over
the Campagna, thinking aloud, as it were.
His mind is full of speculation. What is
become of Rome? — Rome, the home of the
dominant Latin race, born to rule and to
bend other nations to its desires. What is
the Pope? What is the King? Who, who
will combine in himself the triune powers
of passion, intellect, and poetry, and lift the
Italian people back to the saddle of the
world? By severe self-discipline Claudio has
conceived his own life as a whole, as material for art, and has succeeded to so high a
degree that now he holds all his power of
passion, intellect, and poetry like a drawn
sword. He will embody in act the concept
of his life. He reflects how the Nazarene
failed, for he feared the world and knowledge, and turned from them to ignorance
and the desert; how Bonaparte failed, for he
had not the conception of fashioning his life
as a great work of art; and Claudio's mind
turns to his own ancestor, the untimely killed
Alessandro, and ponders that he did not live
and die in vain, but that his spirit still exists,

ready to burst forth in some child of his race. Claudio's duty is to marry a woman who shall bear a son, such that his passion, intellect, and poetry shall make him the redeemer of the world, and restore Rome mistress of nations. As he rides he calls upon the poets to defend the beautiful from the attacks of the gross multitude, and upon the patricians to assume their rightful place as masters of the people, to pick up the fallen whip and frighten back into its sty the Great Beast that grunts in parliament and press.

Filled with these images of his desire, Claudio goes back to his ancestral domain in southern Italy. An aged lord, at one time friend to the last Bourbons of Naples, dwells in a neighboring castle with his three virgin daughters. About this castle we find all the literary devices of Maeterlinck. " The splendor falls on castle walls," but it is a strange light, as of a moon that has overpowered the sun at noon. The genius of the castle is the insane mother, who wanders at will through its chambers, down the paths of its gardens, rustling in her ancient dress, with two gray attendants at her heels. She is hardly seen, but, like a principle of evil,

throws a spell over all the place. In front
of the palace the fountain splashes its waters
in continuous jets into its basin with mur-
murous sounds of mysterious horror. Two
sons hover about, gazing in timid fascina-
tion upon their mother, wondering when the
inheritance of madness shall fall upon them.
One is already doomed; the other, with fearful consciousness, is on the verge of doom.
The three daughters have each her separate
virtue. Massimilla is a likeness of St. Clare,
the companion of St. Francis of Assisi. She
is the spirit of the love that waits and receives. Her heart is a fruitful garden with
an infinite capability for faith. Anatolia is
the spirit of the love that gives. She has
courage, strength, and vitality enough to
comfort and support a host of the weak and
timid. Violante is the tragical spirit of the
power of beauty. The light of triumph and
the beauty of tragedy hang over her like a
veil. From among these three beautiful virgins Claudio must choose one to be the
mother of him who, composed of passion,
power, and poetry, shall redeem the dis-
jointed world, straighten the crooked course
of nature, and set the crown of the world

again on the forehead of Rome. He chooses
Anatolia, and here the book enters the realm
of reality. Anatolia is a real woman; she
feels the duties of womanhood, her bonds to
her father, her mother, and her brothers,
and in a natural and womanly way she re-
fuses to be Claudio's wife. There the book
ends, with the promise of two more volumes.
Anatolia is a living being in this strange
world of fantasy, and though she is not true
to the spirit of the story, she is one of the
indications of d'Annunzio's power.

The faults of the book are great. But
all books are not meant for all persons. Who
shall judge the merits of such a book? The
men who live in a world of action, or the men
who live in a world half made of dreams?
Shakespeare has written "The Tempest" for
both divisions, but other men must be content to choose one or the other. This book
is for the latter class. Yet even for them it
has great faults. The mechanical contriv-
ances, the solitary castle, the insane mother,
the three virgins, the chorus of the fountain,
the iteration of thought, the repetition of
phrase, are all familiar to readers of Maeterlinck. The element of the heroic, the advo-

cacy of a patrician order, the love of Rome,
the adulation of intellectual power, are dis-
cordant with the mysterious nature of the
book. Claudio, full of monster thoughts, —
of a timid Christ, of an ill-rounded Napoleon, of the world's dominion restored to
Rome, — sits down to flirt with Massimilla
in the attitude of a young Baudelaire. The
reader feels that he has been watching a
preraphaelite opera bouffe.

We cannot be without some curiosity as
to what is d'Annunzio's attitude towards his
own novels. In Bourget's " Le Disciple "
we had a hero in very much the same tangle
of psychological theory as is Aurispa. The
disciple wandered far in his search for experience, for new fields and novel combina-
tions of sentiment. His world lost all morality. There was neither right nor wrong in
it, but it still remained a real world. In the
preface, the only chapter in which, under
the present conventionalities of novel-writing, the writer is allowed to speak in his own
voice, Bourget, with Puritan earnestness,
warns the young men of France to beware of
the dangers which he describes, to look forward to the terrible consequences in a world

in which there is neither right nor wrong,
to turn back while yet they may. It seems
reasonable to look to the prefaces to learn
what d'Annunzio's attitude towards his own
books is, and we find no consciousness in
them of right and wrong, of good and evil,
such as troubled Bourget. All d'Annunzio's
work is built upon a separation between humanity — beings knowing good and evil —
and art.

Nevertheless, d'Annunzio has a creed. He
believes in the individual, that he shall take
and keep what he can; that this is no world
in which to play at altruism and to encum-
ber ourselves with hypocrisy. He believes
that power and craft have rights better than
those of weakness and simplicity; that a
chosen race is entitled to all the advantages
accruing from that choice; that a patrician
order is no more bound to consider the lower
classes than men are bound to respect the
rights of beasts. He proclaims this belief,
and preaches to what he regards as the patrician order his mode of obtaining from life
all that it has to give. Art is his watch-
word, the art of life is his text. Know the
beautiful; enjoy all that is new and strange;

be not afraid of the bogies of moral law and of human tradition, — they are idols wrought by ignorant plebeians.

He finds that the main hindrance to the adoption of this creed is an uneasy sense of relativity of life. Even the patrician order entertains a suspicion that life — the noblest material for art to work in — is not of the absolute grain and texture that d'Annunzio's theory presupposes. The individual life, wrought with greatest care, and fashioned into a shape of beauty after d'Annunzio's model, may seem to lose all its loveliness when it is complete and the artist lies on his deathbed. And therefore, in order to obtain disciples, d'Annunzio perceives that he must persuade his patricians to accept the phenomena of life, which the senses present, as final and absolute. The main support for the theory of the relativity of life is religion. In long procession religious creeds troop down through history, and on every banner is inscribed the belief in an Absolute behind the seeming. D'Annunzio must get rid of all these foolish beliefs. He would argue, " They are a train of superstition, ignorance, and fear. They have failed and they will

fail because they dare not face truth. What
is the religious conception of the Divine
love for man, and of the love of man for
God ? God's love is a superstitious infer-
ence drawn from the love of man for God ;
and man's love of God in its turn is but a
blind deduction from man's love for woman.
In the light of science man's love for woman
shrinks to an instinct. This Divine love
that looks so fair, that has made heroes and
sustained mystics, is mere sentimental milli-
nery spun out of a fact of animal life. This
fact is the root of the doctrine of relativity.
From it has sprung religion, idealism, mysticism. Examine this fact scientifically ; see
what it is, and how far, how very far, it is
from justifying the inferences drawn from
love, and without doubt the whole intellectual order of patricians must accept my beliefs." Another man might say : "Suppose
it be so ; suppose this animal fact be the
root from which springs the blossoming tree
of Divine love : this inherent power of
growth dumfounds me more, makes me
more uncertain of my apparent perceptions,
than all the priestly explanations."

In d'Annunzio's idolatry of force there is

a queer lack of the masculine ; his ·voice is
shrill and sounds soprano. In his morbid
supersensitiveness, in his odd fantasy, there
is a feminine strain ; and yet not wholly feminine. In his incongruous delineation of character there is a mingling of hopes and fears,
of thoughts and feelings, that are found
separate and distinct in man and woman.
In all his novels there is an unnatural atmosphere, which is different from that in the
books of the mere *décadents*. There is the
presence of an intellectual and emotional
condition that is neither masculine nor feminine, and yet partaking of both. There is
an appeal to some elements in our nature
of which theretofore we were unaware. As
sometimes on a summer's day, swimming on
the buoyant waters of the ocean, we fancy
that once we were native there, so in reading
this book we have a vague surmise beneath
our consciousness that once there was a time
when the sexes had not been differentiated,
and that we are in ourselves partakers of
the spiritual characteristics of each ; and yet
the feeling is wholly disagreeable. We feel
as if we had been in the secret museum
at Naples, and we are almost ready to bathe

in hot ,lava that we shall no longer feel unclean.

We do not believe that a novel of the first rank can be made out of the materials at d'Annunzio's command. Instead of humor he has scorn and sneer; in place of conscience he gives us swollen egotism; for the deep affections he proffers lust. We are human, we want human beings, and he sets up fantastic puppets; we ask for a man, and under divers aliases he puts forth himself. We grow weary of caparisoned paragraph and bedizened sentence, of clever imitation and brilliant cultivation ; we demand something to satisfy our needs of religion, education, feeling; we want bread, and he gives us a gilded stone. There are great regions of reality and romance still to be discovered by bold adventurers, but Gabriele d'Annunzio will not find them unless he be born again.

MONTAIGNE

MONTAIGNE

I

THERE have been greater men in literature than Montaigne, but none have been more successful. His reputation is immense; he is in men's mouths next to Dante and Cervantes. We look at that intelligent, contemplative, unimpassioned face, with its tired eyes, and wonder that he should have achieved fame as immortal as that of the fierce Italian or the noble Spaniard. In the affairs of fame luck plays its part. Sometimes a man's genius keeps step with his country and his time; he gains power from sympathy, his muscles harden, his head clears, as he runs a winning race. Another man will fail in the enervating atmosphere of recognition and applause; he needs obstacles, the whip and spur of difficulty. Montaigne was born under a lucky star. Had fate shown him all the kingdoms of the world and all time, and given him the choice when and where to live, he could not have chosen better.

Montaigne's genius is French in every
fibre; he embodies better than any one
other man the French character. In this
world nationality counts for much, both at
home and abroad. Frenchmen enjoy their
own; they relish French nature, its niceties,
its strong personality. Sluggish in turning
to foreign things, they are not prone to acquire tastes; but whatever is native to them
they cultivate, study, and appreciate with
rare subtlety. They enjoy Montaigne as
men enjoy a work of art, with the satisfaction of comprehension.

In truth, all men like a strong national
flavor in a book. Montaigne typifies what
France has been to the world: he exhibits
the characteristic marks of French intelligence; he represents the French mind. Of
course such representation is false in many
measures. A nation is too big to have her
character completely shown forth by one man.
Look at the cathedrals of the Ile-de-France;
read the lives of Joan of Arc and St. Francis
of Sales, of the Jesuits in Canada; remember
Liberty, Equality, Fraternity, and that it was,
as M. de Vogüé says, the mad caprice of
France which raised Napoleon to his high

estate; and we realize how fanciful it is to make one man typify a nation. Nevertheless, it is common talk that France takes ideas and makes them clear; that she unravels the tangled threads of thought, eliminating disorder; that she is romantic; that she is not religious; that she shrugs her shoulders at the vague passions of the soul; that she is immensely intelligent; that she is fond of pleasure; and that her favorite diversion is to sit beside the great boulevard of human existence and make comments, fresh, frank, witty, wise.

In these respects Montaigne is typical. He does not create new ideas, he is no explorer; he takes the notions of other men, holds them up to the light, turns them round and about, gazing at them. He is intellectually honest; he dislikes pretense. At bottom, too, he is romantic: witness his reverence for Socrates, his admiration of the Stoics, his desire for the citizenship of Rome. He has the French cast of mind that regards men, primarily, not as individuals, but rather as members of society. He has the sense of behavior. " All strangeness and peculiarity in our manners and ways of life are to be avoided as enemies to society. . . . Knowledge of how to behave in company is a very useful knowledge. Like grace and beauty, it conciliates at the very beginning of acquaintance, and in consequence opens the door for us to learn by the example of others, and to set an example ourselves, if we have anything worth teaching."

Montaigne is not religious, — certainly not after the fashion of a Bishop Brooks or a Father Hecker. He is a pagan rather than a Christian. He likes gayety, wit, agreeable society; he is fond of conversation. He boards his subject like a sociable creature, he is a born talker, he talks away obscurity. He follows his subject as a young dog follows a carriage, bounding off the road a hundred times to investigate the neighborhood. His loose-limbed mind is easy, light, yet serious. He pares away the rind of things, smelling the fruit joyously, not as if employed in a business of funereal looks, but in something human and cheerful. He has good taste.

Montaigne had good luck not only in his country, but also in his generation. He lived at the time when the main current of

Latin civilization shifted from Italy to France. In the beginning of the sixteenth century, Italy was the intellectual head of the Latin world, her thought and art were the moulding forces of modern civilization. When the seventeenth century opened, France had assumed the primacy. The great culmination of the Italian Renaissance came close to the time of Montaigne's birth; when he died, Italy was sinking into dependence in thought and servility in art, whereas France was emerging from her civil wars, under the rule of one of the greatest of Frenchmen, ready to become the dominant power, politically and intellectually, in Europe. Coming at this time, Montaigne was a pioneer. His was one of the formative minds which gave to French intelligence that temper which has enabled it to do so much for the world in the last three hundred years. He showed it a great model of dexterity, lightness, and ease.

Not only did Montaigne help fashion the French intelligence in that important period, but he did much to give that intelligence a tool by which it could put its capacities to use. It is from Montaigne that French prose gets a buoyant lightness. He has

been called one of the great French poets.
Had it not been for Montaigne and his contemporaries, the depressing influence of the
seventeenth century would have hardened
the language, taking out its grace, and making it a clever mechanical contrivance. His
influence has been immense. It is said that
an hundred years after his death his Essays
were to be found on the bookshelves of
every gentleman in France. French critics
trace his influence on Pascal, La Bruyère,
Rousseau, Montesquieu, Sainte-Beuve, and
Renan. To-day no one can read M. Anatole
France or M. Jules Lemaître without saying
to himself, " This is fruit from the same rich
stock."

There are reasons besides these which
have given Montaigne his great position in
the world's literature. The first is his habit
of mind. He is a considerer, an examiner, a
skeptic. He prowls about the beliefs, the
opinions and usages, of men, and, taking up
a thought, lifts from it, one by one, the
envelopes of custom, of prejudice, of time,
of place. He holds up the opinion of one
school, praising and admiring it ; and then
the contradictory opinion of another school,

praising and admiring that. In his scales he balances notion against notion, man against man, usage against usage. It was his great usefulness that, in a time when notable men put so much trust in matters of faith that they constructed theologies of adamant and burnt dissenters, he calmly announced the relativity of knowledge. He was no student mustily thinking in a dead language, but a gentleman in waiting to the king, knight of the Order of St. Michael, writing in fresh, poetic French, with all the captivation of charm, teaching the fundamental principles of doubt and uncertainty; for if there be doubt there will be tolerance, if there be uncertainty there will be liberality. He laid the axe to the root of religious bigotry and civil intolerance. " Things apart by themselves have, it may be, their weight, their dimensions, their condition ; but within us, the mind cuts and fashions them according to its own comprehension. . . . Health, conscience, authority, knowledge, riches, beauty, and their contraries, strip off their outward semblances at the threshold of the mind, and receive at its hands new garments, of such dyes as it please."

The emphasis of self is at the base of modern life. The art of the Renaissance sprung from the passion for self-expression. The Reformation took self as the hammer which broke the yoke of the Roman Church. Self stood on its feet and faced God; what need of priests and intermediaries? Montaigne is a great exponent of this spirit. A man of letters and a philosopher, he did not find in duty an explanation of life, but he realized the significance of this imperious self, this I, I, I, that proclaims itself to be at the bottom of everything. Step by step, as he goes from Plato to Cicero, from Cicero to Seneca, from Seneca to Plutarch, he discovers humanity taking individual form; compressed into the likeness of a single man, it puts on familiar features, it speaks with a well-known voice, turns and shapes itself in the mould of a single human mind: that face, that voice, that mind, are his own. Start how he will, every road twists and winds back to himself. As if by compulsion he gradually renounces all other study. In self is to be found the philosophy of life. If we once firmly accept the notion that we know nothing but ourselves, then the universe outside becomes a

shadowy collection of vapors, mysterious, hy-
pothetical, and self hardens into the only
reality. Here is a basis for a religion or a
philosophy. So speculating, the philosopher
opened the eyes of the artist. If self be the
field of philosophy, it is the opportunity of
the artist. Never had a man of letters sat
to himself for his own portrait. Montaigne
is the "prince of egotists," because he is a
philosopher and a great artist. He is a skeptic, but he points a way to positive doctrine.
He is a man of letters, but he teaches the
primary rules of civil and religious liberty.
He is a member of the Holy Church, Apostolic and Roman, but he lays the foundation
of a philosophy open to Reformer and to
infidel. Profoundly interested in the questions lying at the base of life, he is one of
the greatest artists of the Renaissance.

II

Montaigne was a Gascon, of a family of
merchants. His great-grandfather, Ramon
Eyquem, founded the family fortunes by
trade, and bettered them by a prudent marriage. He became one of the richest merchants of Bordeaux, dealing in wine and salt

fish, and bought the estate of Montaigne, a little seigniory near the river Dordogne, not very far from the city. His son, Grimon, also prospered, and in his turn left to his son, Pierre, Montaigne's father, so good a property that Pierre was enabled to give up trade, and betake himself to arms. Pierre served for several years in Italy, under Francis I. On his return he married Antoinette de Louppes, or Lopes, a rich lady of Spanish descent, with some Jewish blood in her veins. He was an active, hard-working, conscientious, capable man, devoting himself to public affairs. He held one office after another in the city of Bordeaux, and finally was elected mayor. He took especial interest in education, improving the schools, and making changes for the better in the college. His interest amounted to a hobby, if we may judge from his method of educating his son. His years in Italy had opened his mind, and though no scholar himself, he was a great admirer of the new learning, and sought the company of scholars. Evidently, he was a man who liked to think, and was not afraid to put his ideas into practice. He enlarged the seigniory of Montaigne and rebuilt the château. His son says

of him that he was the best father that ever
was; that he was ambitious to do everything
that was honorable, and had a very high regard for his word.

Michel was born on the last day of Febru-
ary, 1533. He was the third of eleven children; the two elder died in infancy. His
education began at once. Still a baby, he
was put in charge of some peasants who
lived near the château, in order that his
earliest notions should be of simple things.
His god-parents were country folk; for Pierre
Eyquem deemed it better that his son should
early learn to make friends " with those who
stretch their arms toward us rather than with
those who turn their backs on us." The second step in education was to direct Michel's
mind so that it should naturally take the heroic Roman mould. His father thought that
this result would be more likely to follow
if the baby spoke Latin. He was therefore
put into the hands of a learned German, who
spoke Latin very well, and could speak no
French. There were also two other scholars
in attendance on the little boy, — less learned,
however, — who took turns with the German
in accompanying him. They also spoke no-

thing but Latin in Michel's presence. " As
for the rest of the household, it was an in-
violable rule that neither my father nor
mother, nor the man servant nor the maid
servant, should speak when I was by, except
some Latin words which they had learned
on purpose to talk with me." This rule was
so well obeyed that not only his father and
mother learned enough Latin to understand
it and to speak it a little, but also the servants who waited on him. In fact, they all
became so very Latin that even the people
in the village called various implements and
utensils by their Latin names. Montaigne
was more than six years old before he heard
any French spoken; he spoke Latin as if it
were his native tongue.

At six Montaigne was sent to the College
of Guyenne, in Bordeaux, where his Latin
began to get bad, and served no better purpose than to make his studies so easy that
he was quickly put into the higher classes.
He stayed at college till he had completed
the course in 1546, when he was thirteen
years old. He says that he took no knowledge of any value away with him. This
statement must be taken with a grain of

salt, for he had been under the care of famous scholars, and instead of wasting his
time over poor books or in idleness he had
read the best Latin authors. He did not
even know the name of Amadis of Gaul, but
fell upon Ovid, Virgil, Terence, and Plautus.
After them he read the Italian comedies.
This reading was done on the sly, the teachers winking at it. " Had they not done so,"
he says, " I should have left college with a
hatred for books, like almost all the young
nobility."

Whether or not, so bred, Montaigne became more like Scipio and Cato Major, his
father's interest in education no doubt stim-
ulated his own. In all the shrewdness of
the Essays there is no more definite and
practical teaching than his advice on education, especially in his asseverations of its
large purposes. " There is nothing so noble," he says, " as to make a man what he
should be ; there is no learning comparable
to the knowledge of how to live this life
aright and according to the laws of nature."
Montaigne laid down, clearly and sharply,
principles that sound commonplace to-day :
that the object of education is to make, not

a scholar, but a man; that education shall
concern itself with the understanding rather
than with the memory; that mind and body
must be developed together. It would be
easy to quote pages. "To know by heart is
not to know; it is only holding on to what
has been put into the custody of the memory.
. . . We receive as bailiffs the opinions and
learning of others; we must make them our
own. . . . We learn to say Cicero says this,
Plato thinks this, these are Aristotle's words;
but we, what do *we* say? What do we do?
What is our opinion? . . . If the mind does
not acquire a better temper, if the judgment
does not become more sound, I had as lief
the schoolboy should pass his time playing
tennis: his body, at least, would be more sup-
ple. See him come back after years spent:
there is nothing so unfit for use; all that
you see more than he had before is that
his Latin and Greek leave him more silly
and conceited than when he left home. He
ought to have brought back a full mind: he
brings it back blown out; instead of having
it bigger, it is only puffed up. . . . It is also
an opinion accepted by everybody that a boy
ought not to be brought up round his parents'

knees. Natural affection makes them too tender and too soft; they are not able to punish his faults, nor to see him nourished hardily, as he should be, and run risks. They won't let him come back sweating and dusty from exercise, drink hot, drink cold, nor see him on a horse backwards, nor facing a rough fencer foil in hand, nor with his first gun. There's no help for it: if you wish to make a man, you must not spare him such matters of youth. You must often break the rules of medicine. It is not enough to make his soul firm; his muscles must be firm too. The soul is too hard pressed if she be not supported well, and has too much to do if she must furnish strength for both."

Montaigne himself must have learned the value of exercise, for he became a great horseman, more at home on horseback than on foot. Till the time of ill health he seems to have had a vigorous body; he could sit in the saddle for eight or ten hours, and survived a very severe fall, though he " vomited buckets of blood."

Of Montaigne's life after leaving the college we know little or nothing. He must have studied law, — perhaps at the University of Toulouse, perhaps in Bordeaux. But matters other than the classics or civil law, and more profitable to a great critic of life, must have been rumbling in his ears, making him begin to speculate on the opinions and customs of men, and their reasonableness. Already troubles prophetic of civil war were afoot.

III

In 1554 the king established a Court of Aids at Périgueux. Pierre Eyquem was appointed one of the magistrates, but before he took his seat he was elected mayor of Bordeaux, and resigned his position as member of the court in favor of his son, who, under the system then prevalent, became magistrate in his stead. Montaigne was twenty-one years old. After a year or two the Court of Aids was annulled, and its magistrates were made members of the Parlement of Bordeaux. Here Montaigne met Etienne de La Boétie, who was also a member. The two men at once became most loving friends. La Boétie had a noble, passionate character. Montaigne says that he was cast in the heroic mould, an antique

Roman, the greatest man of their time. After six years La Boétie died, in 1563. Seventeen years later, while traveling in Italy, Montaigne wrote to a friend, " All of a sudden I fell to thinking about M. de La Boétie, and I stayed so long without shaking the fit off that it made me feel very sad." This was the master affection of Montaigne's life, and the noblest. It was a friendship " so whole, so perfect, that there are none such to be read of, and among men to-day there is no trace to be seen. There is need of so happy a meeting to fashion it that fortune does well if it happens once in three hundred years." They were wont to call each other " brother." " In truth, the name of brother is beautiful and full of sweetness; for this reason he and I gave it to the bond between us."

La Boétie died of the plague, or some disease like it. He told Montaigne that his illness was contagious, and besought him to stay with him no more than a few minutes at a time, but as often as he could. From that time Montaigne never left him. This act must be remembered, if we incline to blame Montaigne for shunning Bordeaux when the plague was upon it.

Two years afterwards Montaigne married Françoise de la Chassaigne. It was a match made from considerations of suitability. The Eyquems were thrifty wooers. Montaigne had no romantic notions about love in marriage; he did not seek a "Cato's daughter" who should help him climb the heights of life. He says: "The most useful and honorable knowledge and occupation for a mother of a family is the knowledge of housekeeping. That should be a woman's predominant attribute; that is what a man should look for when he goes a-courting. From what experience has taught me, I should require of a wife, above all other virtues, that of the housewife." Nevertheless, they were very happily married. She was a woman of good sense and ability, and looked after the affairs of the seigniory with a much quicker eye than her husband. He dedicated to her a translation made by La Boétie from Plutarch. "Let us live," he says, "you and me, after the old French fashion. . . . I do not think I have a friend more intimate than you."

Montaigne remained magistrate for fifteen years. He did not find the duties very much

to his taste, but he must have acquitted
himself well, because a year or two after his
retirement the king decorated him with the
Order of St. Michael. These years of his
magistracy were calm enough for Montaigne,
but they were not calm for France. In 1562
the civil wars broke out. There is something too fish-blooded about a man who sits
in the "back of his shop" and attends to
his judicial duties or writes essays, clammily
watching events, while the country is on fire.
But what has a skeptic to do with divine
rights of kings or divine revelations?

Little by little Montaigne was getting
ready to forsake the magistracy for literature.
He began by translating, at his father's wish,
the "Theologia Naturalis" of Raymond de
Sebonde, — a treatise which undertook to
establish the truth of the Christian religion
by a process of reasoning. His father died
before he finished it. It was published in
1569. The next year Montaigne resigned
his seat in the Parlement of Bordeaux, and
devoted himself to the publication of various
manuscripts left by La Boétie. This done,
the new Seigneur de Montaigne — he dropped
the unaristocratic name of Eyquem — retired

to his seigniory, "with a resolution to avoid
all manner of concern in affairs as much as
possible, and to spend the small remainder
of his life in privacy and peace." There he
lived for nine years, riding over his estates,
planting, tending, — or more wisely suffering his wife to superintend, — receiving his
friends, hospitable, enjoying opportunities
to talk, or more happy still in his library.
Here, in the second story of his tower, shut
off from the buzz of household life, his
friends, Plutarch, Cicero, Seneca, Herodotus,
Plato, with a thousand volumes more, on the
shelves, the ceiling carved with aphorisms,
Latin and Greek, he used to sit fulfilling his
inscription : "In the year of Christ 1571, at
the age of thirty-eight, on his birthday, the
day before the calends of March, Michel de
Montaigne, having quitted some time ago
the servitude of courts and public duties,
has come, still in good health, to rest among
the Muses. In peace and safety he will pass
here what days remain for him to live, in the
hope that the Fates will allow him to perfect
this habitation, this sweet paternal asylum
consecrated to independence, tranquillity,
and leisure."

IV

It was quiet in the Château de Montaigne; Plutarch and Cicero sat undisturbed, except for notes scribbled on their margins; but in Paris the Duke of Guise and the royal house were making St. Bartholomew a memorable day. Civil war again ravaged France, the League conspired with Spain, Henry of Navarre rallied the Huguenots, while the king, Henry III., dangled between them, making and breaking edicts. The Seigneur de Montaigne rode about his estates, or sat in his library, writing "Concerning Idleness," "Concerning Pedantry," "Concerning Coaches," "Concerning Solitude," "Concerning Sumptuary Laws."

The most apathetic of us, knowing that Henry of Navarre and Henry of Guise are in the field, become so many Hotspurs at the thought of this liberal-minded gentleman, the Order of St. Michael hanging round his neck, culling anecdotes out of Plutarch about Cyrus or Scipio. "Zounds! how has he leisure to be sick in such a justling time!" We readers are a whimsical people; cushioned in armchairs, we catch on

fire at the white plume of Navarre. What
is the free play of thought to us?   Give us
sword and pistol, — *Ventre-Saint-Gris!* But
the best fighting has not been done on bat-
tlefields, and Montaigne has helped the cause
of justice and humanity better than twenty
thousand armed men.

Once, when there does not seem to have
been an immediate prospect of a fight, Montaigne offered his services to one of the
king's generals.   Instead of being ordered
to the field, he was sent back to Bordeaux
to harangue the Parlement on the need of
new fortifications.   He was a loyal servant
of the king, and deemed the Huguenots a
rebellious faction, fighting against lawful authority; but his heart could not take sides;
he was disgusted with the hypocrisy of both
parties, and the mask of religion.   "I see
it is evident that we render only those offices
to piety which tickle our passions.   There is
no enmity so excellent as the Christian.   Our
zeal does wonders, when it goes following
our inclination toward hate, cruelty, ambition, avarice, detraction, rebellion.   But the
converse, — toward goodness, kindness, temperance, — if, as by miracle, some rare con-

junction takes it that way, it goes neither
afoot nor with wings. Our religion was
made to pluck out vices; it uncovers them,
nurses them, encourages them. . . . Let us
confess the truth: he that should pick out
from the army, even the loyal army, those
who march there only for zeal of religious
feeling, and also those who singly consider
the maintenance of their country's laws or
the service of their sovereign, he could not
make a corporal's guard of them."

Montaigne was a Catholic. He did not
share that passionate care of conduct which
animated the Reformers. He did not see
that the truth of a religion was affected by
the misbehavior of its priests. When he
heard, in Rome, that " the general of the
Cordeliers had been deprived of his place,
and locked up, because in a sermon, in presence of the Pope and the cardinals, he had
accused the prelates of the Church of lazi-
ness and ostentation, without particularity,
only, speaking in commonplaces, on this subject," Montaigne merely felt that civil liberty had been abused. He was not troubled
to find the ceremonies in St. Peter's " more
magnificent than devotional," nor to learn

that the Pope, Gregory XIII., had a son.
He was amused at the luxurious ways of the
cardinals. He made the acquaintance of the
maître d'hôtel of Cardinal Caraffa. "I made
him tell me of his employment. He discoursed on the science of the gullet with the
gravity and countenance of a judge, as if
he had been talking of some grave point of
theology ; he deciphered a difference of appetites, — that which one has when hungry,
that which one has after the second and
after the third course ; the means first merely
to please it, then to wake it and prick it ;
the policy of sauces," etc. He heard on the
portico of St. Peter's a canon of the Church
" read aloud a Latin bull, by which an immense number of people were excommuni-
cated, among others the Huguenots, by that
very name, and all princes who withheld
any of the lands of the Church. At this
article the cardinals, Medici and Caraffa, who
were next to the Pope, laughed very hard."
The Master of the Sacred Palace had subjected the Essays to examination, and found
fault with Montaigne's notion that torture in
addition to death was cruelty. Montaigne
replied that he did not know that the opinion

was heretical. To his mind, such matters
had nothing to do with truth or religion.
He accepted the Apostolic Roman Catholic
faith. He was not disposed to take a single
step out of the fold. If one, why not two?
And if reason once mutinied and took control, where would it stop? He denied the
competence of human reason to investigate.
things divine. " Man can only be what he
is; he can only imagine according to his
measure."

To a man who took pleasure in travels,
foibles, whims, philosophy, to a man of the
Renaissance full of eagerness to study the
ancients and to enjoy them, to a man by no
means attracted by the austerities of the Cal-
vinists, a war for the sake of supplanting the
old religion of France was greatly distaste-
ful. He could not but admit that the Huguenots were right so far as they only wished
liberty of worship, nor fail to respect their
obedience to conscience. But his heart had
not the heroic temper; he wanted peace,
comfort, scholarship, elegance. It is one
thing to sit in a library and admire heroic
men in the pages of Plutarch, and another
to enjoy living in the midst of them.

Montaigne spent these years in pleasant peacefulness, dawdling over his library, and putting his Essays together scrap by scrap. In 1580, at the age of forty-seven, he published the first two books of his Essays, which had an immediate and great success. After this he was obliged to forego literature for a time, because he was not well. He had little confidence in doctors, but hoped that he could get benefit by drinking natural waters. Therefore he went traveling. He also wanted to see the world : Rome, with which he had been familiar from boyhood, and Italy, of which he had heard so much from his father, and all strange lands. Perhaps, too, he was not unmindful that he was now not only the Seigneur de Montaigne, but the first man of letters in France, not even excepting Ronsard. He set forth in the summer of 1580, with his brother and several friends, journeying on horseback to Switzerland, Germany, and Italy. He kept a journal, which contains notes of travel, and also a full account of the effects of medicinal waters on his health. The interest of the journal consists chiefly in the pictures of those countries at that time, sketched by an intelligent traveler; but now and again there is a more personal interest, when Montaigne sees something that excites his curiosity. There is a likeness in his curiosity for foreign lands and his curiosity for ideas. He travels into Germany as if it were a new volume of Plutarch. He is agog for novelty, and new ways of life, new points of view. His secretary says: " I never saw him less tired nor less complaining of ill health; he was in high spirits both traveling and stopping, so absorbed in what he met, and always looking for opportunities to talk to strangers. . . . I think if he had been alone with his servants he would have gone to Cracow or to Greece overland, rather than directly into Italy."

In this journal, written first at his direction, perhaps at his dictation, by a secretary, and then, with some inconvenience, as he says, by himself, we find his interests and affections in the light and shadow of the first impression. In the Essays every paragraph is the cud of long rumination. Of Rome the journal says: " We see nothing of Rome but the sky under which she lies and the place of her abode ; knowledge of her is an abstraction, framed by thought, with which the senses have no concern. Those who say that the ruins of Rome at least are to be seen say too much, for the ruins of so tremendous a fabric would bring more honor and reverence to her memory; here is nothing but her place of burial. The world, hostile to her long dominion, has first broken and dashed to pieces all the parts of that admirable body; and because, even when dead, overthrown and mutilated, she still made the world afraid, it has buried even the ruins. The little show of them that appears above the sepulchre has been preserved by fortune, to bear witness to that matchless grandeur which centuries, conflagrations, conspiracies of a world again and again plotting its ruin, have failed to destroy utterly."

Rome, " the noblest city that ever was or ever will be," had laid hold of his imagination. He says, " I used all the five senses that nature gave me to obtain the title of Roman Citizen, if it were only for the ancient honor and religious memory of its authority." By the help of a friend, the Pope's influence procured him this dignity. The decree, bearing the S. P. Q. R., " pompous with seals and gilt letters," gave him great pleasure.

He showed special interest in strange customs, as in the rite of circumcision, and in a ceremony of exorcising an evil spirit. This examination of other ways of living, other habits of thought, is the lever by which he lifts himself out of prejudices, out of the circle of authority, into his free and open-minded state. He always wished to see men who looked at life from other points of view. In Rome, as his secretary writes, " M. de Montaigne was vexed to find so many Frenchmen there; he hardly met anybody in the street who did not greet him in his own tongue." In the Essays Montaigne says that, for education, acquaintance with men is wonderfully good, and also to travel in foreign lands; not to bring back (after the fashion of the French nobility) nothing but the measures of the Pantheon, but to take home a knowledge of foreign ways of thought and of behavior, and to rub and polish our minds against those of others.

V

While abroad, Montaigne received word, in September, 1581, that he had been elected mayor of Bordeaux, to succeed the Maréchal de Biron. He hesitated, he had no mind to give up his freedom; but the king sent an order, flattering and peremptory, that he should betake himself to his office " without delay or excuse," and accordingly he went.

It seems likely that there was some hand behind the scenes which pointed out to the councilors a man who would be acceptable to persons in high place. The Maréchal de Biron wished to be reëlected, but both the king and Henry of Navarre, the nominal governor of Guyenne, were opposed to him. History does not tell what happened, but the mayoralty was given to this distinguished, quiet gentleman, who had kept carefully aloof from partisanship. The office of mayor was not very burdensome; the ordinary duties of administration fell upon others. Montaigne's first term of two years passed uneventfully. De Thou, the historian, who knew him at this time, says that he learned much from Montaigne, a man " very well

versed in public affairs, especially in those
concerning Guyenne, which he knows thoroughly." In 1583 he was reëlected. Times
grew more troubled. On the death of the
king's brother, Navarre became heir to the
throne. The League, alarmed, made new
efforts. Guise made a secret treaty with
Spain that Navarre should not be recognized
as king. Coming storms began to blow up
about Bordeaux. The League plotted to
seize the city. Poor Montaigne found himself in the midst of excursions and alarms.
He was glad to lay down his charge when
his term ended, on July 31, 1585. In June
a horrible plague broke out, while Montaigne
was away, and people in Bordeaux died by
hundreds. The council asked him to come
to town to preside over the election of his
successor. He answered, " I will not spare
my life or anything in your service, and I
leave you to judge whether what I can do
for you by my presence at the next election
makes it worth while for me to run the risk
of going to town." The council did not insist, and Montaigne did not go. This is the
act of his life which has called forth blame,
not from his contemporaries, but from stout-

hearted critics and heroic reviewers. To set
an example of indifference to death is outside the ordinary path of duty. We like to
hear tell of splendid recklessness of life, of
fools who go to death out of a mad desire
to stamp the fear of it under their feet; and
when disappointed of so fine a show, we become petulant, we betray that we are over-
fond of excitement. It was not the mayor's
duty to look after the public health; that
lay upon the council.

His office ended, Montaigne went back to
his library, to revise and correct the first
two books of his Essays, to stuff them with
new paragraphs and quotations, and to write
a third. But he could not retire far enough
to get away from the sounds of civil war.
Coutras was but a little too far for him to
hear Navarre harangue his troops to victory,
and the voices of the soldiers singing the
psalm : —

> "This is the day which the Lord hath made
> We will rejoice and be glad in it."

A few days afterwards Henry of Navarre
stopped at the château and dined with Montaigne. He had once before been there,
making a visit of two days, when Montaigne

was still mayor. The relations of these two
men are interesting, but somewhat difficult
to decipher. De Thou relates that Montaigne talked to him about Henry of Navarre
and the Duke of Guise, and their hatred one
of the other, and said : " As for religion,
both make parade of it; it is a fine pretext
to make those of their party follow them.
But the interest of religion does n't touch
either of them; only the fear of being abandoned by the Protestants prevents the king
of Navarre from returning to the religion of
his ancestors, and the duke would betake
himself to the Augsburg Confession, for
which his uncle, Charles, Cardinal of Lor-
raine, had given him a taste, if he could
follow it without prejudice to his interests."
But Navarre, though he was open-minded
on the subject of creeds, and a most dexter-
ous politician, was a noble and loyal gentleman, as Montaigne, with his keen, unpreju-
diced eyes, could well see. Navarre had
been bred a Protestant, his friends were Protestants, and he would not forswear his religion so long as abjuration might work harm
to them. When his conversion became of
great moment to France, and promised to

confer the blessings of peace on the country without hurt to the Protestants, he turned Catholic. This was conduct such as Montaigne would most heartily approve. Henry IV. acted as if he had been nursed on the Essays. And there is much to show that De Thou's conversation is a very incorrect account of Montaigne's opinion of Henry.

After Henry had succeeded to the throne, and was still struggling with the League, Montaigne wrote to him: "I have always thought of you as enjoying the good fortune to which you have come, and you may remember that, even when I was obliged to confess it to the curé, I always hoped for your success. Now, with more cause and more freedom, I salute it with full affection. Your success serves you where you are, but it serves you no less here by reputation. The noise does as much as the shot. We could not draw from the justice of your cause arguments to establish or win your subjects so strong as we do from the news of the prosperity of your enterprises. . . . The inclinations of people flow in a tide. If the incline is once in your favor, it will sweep on of its own weight, to the very end.

I should have liked very much that the private gain of your soldiers and the need of making them content had not deprived you, especially in this great city, of the noble commendation of having treated your rebellious subjects, in the hour of victory, with more consideration than their own protectors do ; and that, differently from a transitory and usurped claim, you had shown that they were yours by a fatherly and truly royal protection." The letter shows admiration and comprehension of the king, and an intimacy honorable to both. There was some invitation for Montaigne to come to court, and an offer of money, but he answered : "Sire, your Majesty will do me, if you please, the favor to believe that I will never stint my purse on an occasion for which I would not spare my life. I have never received any money from the liberality of kings, — I have neither asked nor deserved it ; I have never received payment for the steps I have taken in their service, of which your Majesty in part has knowledge. What I have done for your predecessors I will do very much more willingly for you. I am, Sire, as rich as I desire." But ill health would not permit him to go, even if he had wished.

In the mean time Montaigne had been in Paris (in 1588) to publish a new edition of the Essays.   There he formed the acquaintance of Mademoiselle de Gournay, a young lady of twenty, who had conceived a great enthusiasm for the Essays. Montaigne called her his adopted daughter.   After his death, helped by Madame de Montaigne, she devoted herself to the preparation of a new edition of the Essays, with all the last changes and additions that the author had made.

Montaigne spent the last few years of his life on his seigniory.   He lived quietly, his health growing worse, till he died, on September 13, 1592, at the age of fifty-nine.   It is said that when he felt his death near, no longer able to speak, he wrote a little note asking his wife to summon several gentlemen of the neighborhood, that he might take leave of them.   When they had come, he had mass said in his room ; and when the priest came to the elevation of the host, he threw himself forward as best he could, his hands clasped, and so died.

VI

We are wont to call a man of letters great when many generations of men can go to his book, read what he says on the subject that concerns them, — conduct, religion, love, the significance of life, — and find that he has cast some light, or at least has shifted the problem. Such is Montaigne. There were greater men living in his time, Shakespeare, Cervantes; but life plies many questions to which poetry and idealism give no direct answer. If a man would look serenely upon the world, and learn the lesson that "ripeness is all," he must go to the poet and to the idealist, but he must go to the skeptic, too. Uncertainty is one of our lessons, and what man has talked so wisely and so persuasively as Montaigne concerning matters that lie at the threshold of the great questions of religion and philosophy, which must underlie all reasonable life? Hear him, for instance, after finding fault with an excessive credulity, blaming its opposite : "But also, on the other part, it is presumptuous and foolish to go about disdaining and condemning as false that which does not seem

probable to us. This is a vice common to
those who think they have an intelligence
out of the ordinary. I had that habit once,
and if I heard of ghosts or prophecies of
future events, or of magic, of witchcraft, or
some wonderful story which I could not en-
dure, I felt compassion for the poor people
abused by this nonsense. Now I find that
I myself was at least as much to be pitied.
Not that I have ever had any experience beyond my first beliefs, and nothing has ever
appealed to my curiosity ; but reason has
taught me that to condemn finally a thing
as false and impossible is to claim to comprehend the boundaries and limits of the
will of God and of the power of our mother
Nature, and that there is no more remarkable folly in the world than to bring them
down to the measurements of our capacity
and intelligence. If we give the names
monsters or miracles, there where our reason cannot go, how many continually come
before our eyes ? Consider in what a mist,
and how gropingly, we come to a knowledge
of most things that are under our hands ;
we shall find that it is familiarity, not knowledge, which has taken the strangeness away,

and that, if those things were presented to us afresh, we should find them as much or more unbelievable than any others."

Montaigne commends us to a prudent but brave open-mindedness. He warns us against the dogmas of affirmation and the dogmas of denial. He bids us pause and consider. Nothing could be more wrong than the vulgar notion that Montaigne has something in common with Mephistopheles, the spirit that denies. He was a skeptic; but a single epithet is always incorrect. He was a believer, too. He believed in education, in humanity, in tolerance, in the many-sidedness of life, in the infinite power of God, in the nobleness of humanity. Nothing excites his indignation so violently as the "great subtlety" of those men who sneer at heroic deeds, and attribute noble performance to mean motives. He makes no pretense of special interest in conduct; but conduct is not his business, — he is concerned with the philosophy which underlies conduct. Some men are impatient for action; they will believe this, that, anything, for an excuse to be up and doing. Montaigne is not a man of action; he feels uncomfortable when within

hearing of the whir and rush of life; he
likes to retire into the "back of his shop"
to get away and be quiet. He was for contemplation and meditation. It was this
shrinking from action that made him a skeptic. Action is the affirmation of belief, but
also its begetter. I believe because I act.
The heart beats, the blood circulates, the
breath comes and goes, the impatient muscles
do not wait for the tardy reason to don hat
and overcoat, arms twitch, legs start, and the
man is plunged into the hurly-burly of life.
There he goes, in the midst of a crowd of
human beings, hurrying, struggling, squirm-
ing, all filled to surfeit with most monstrous
beliefs. Montaigne's heart beats more slowly;
he is in no hurry to act; the meaning of
life will not yield to mere importunity; let
us keep cool. "If any difficulties occur in
reading, I do not bite my nails about them,
but, after an attempt or two to explain them,
I give them over. Should I insist upon
them, I should lose both myself and my
time; for I have a genius that is extremely
volatile, and what I do not discern at the
first attempt becomes the more obscure to
me the longer I pore over it. . . . Continua-

tion and a too obstinate contention stupefy and tire my judgment. I must withdraw it, and leave it, to make new discoveries, just as, in order to judge rightly of the lustre of scarlet, we are ordered to pass it lightly with the eye, and to run it over at several sudden repeated views."

Montaigne is of the Latin people, men of the south, children of the market place and the piazza. He sits in peacefulness, watching the comedy and tragedy of the world. He lives apart; for him life is a show, a school for philosophy, a subject for essays. If you have been bred in the Adirondacks or on the slope of Monadnock, up betimes, to tire your legs all the long day, and at evening to watch the setting sun and listen for the first call of the owl, you will not like Montaigne. There, in the morning of life, the blue sky overhead, the realities of life looking so strong and so noble, the speculations of a skeptic come like a cloud of dust. Montaigne is not for the young man. Youth has convictions; its feelings purport absolute verity; it possesses reality: why go a-fishing for dreams? But when the blood runs cooler, when we are glad to be safe on earth,

when of a winter's evening we listen to the
pleasant shoot of the bolt that shall keep us
to ourselves, and draw up to the fire, then
Montaigne is supreme. He is so agreeable,
so charming, so skillful in taking up one
subject, then another, so well practiced in
conversation, so perfect a host. We are
translated into his library. He wanders
about the room, taking from his shelves one
book after another, opening them at random,
reading a scrap, and then talking about it.
On he goes, talking wisely, wittily, kindly,
while the flickering firelight plays over his
sensitive, intelligent face, and the Gascon
moon shines in patches on the floor, till the
world we are used to dissolves under his
talk, and its constituent parts waver and
flicker with the firelight. Everything aërifies
into dream-made stuff, out of which our fancy
builds a new world, only to see it again dis-
solve and fade under his bewitching talk.

Montaigne talks of himself. But his self
is not the vulgar self of the gossip ; it is the
type and model of humanity. Like a great
artist, he makes himself both individual and
type. He is the psychologist studying man.
He is his own laboratory, his own object of

examination. When we try to discover the
movements of the mind, have we any choice?
Must we not examine ourselves? He does
not bring us to himself for the mere exhilaration of talking about himself. His subject
is man ; through the windows of man's mind
he makes us gaze at the universe, forever
reiterating in our ears that man is a prisoner
in the four walls of his mind, chafe how he
will. If this be egotism, it is egotism with
all its teeth drawn.

Skeptic, philosopher, abstracted from the
world, Montaigne nevertheless does not shirk
when the choice comes between speaking
out and keeping silent. He had something
sturdy at bottom. We cannot repeat too
often his " We must rend the mask from
things as well as from men." This is no
easy task. Even the strength of the young
mountaineer may not suffice. Masks familiar to us all our lives become very dear ; let
us leave them, — there are other things to
do. Is there not something ignoble in this
use of our courage, to maltreat an old, venerable appearance? Give us some work of
poetry and romance ; bid us scale heaven.
And so the masks of things remain unre-

moved. There is in Montaigne always the admiration of the heroic. "All other knowledge is useless to him who does not know how to be good. . . . The measure and the worth of a man consist in his heart and will; in them is the home of his honor. . . . True victory lieth in the fight, not in coming off safely; and the honor of courage is in combat, not in success." Of the three philosophies which he studied, the Epicurean, the Pyrrhonian, the Stoic, his heart was inclined to the last, and I think he would rather have had a nod of approval from Cato the younger than have heard Sainte-Beuve salute him as the wisest of Frenchmen.

MACAULAY

MACAULAY

I

THE history of England is the great romance of the modern world. The story of the rise, triumph, decline and fall of the Roman Empire is more dramatic; it would be impossible to match in interest the narrative of that Roman people from their cradle on the Palatine Hill until they walked abroad masters of the world. But England is now living in the height of her pride and power, the great civilizing force of this century. Sprung from the mingled blood of Celt, Saxon, Scandinavian, and Norman, the Englishman has made his island home a garden of poetry, a school of government for the nations, the factory of the world :—

> " This happy breed of men, this little world ;
> This precious stone set in the silver sea."

The story of England outdoes the Waverley Novels. Its panorama extends like the visions of an enchanter : the mightiest Julius

lands ; legionaries build walls and camps, and
withdraw ; wild men struggle with wild men ;
missionaries teach the Pater Noster to awk-
ward lips ; petty kingdoms weld together ;
Saxons strike down Celts ; Normans strike
down Saxons ; Crusaders cross the seas ; Run-
nymede listens to a great charter ; English
judges and English priests struggle against
the dominion of Roman law and Roman theology ; Hotspurs and Warwicks march across
the stage ; sons of serfs are born free men ,
English kings lay claims to the lands of
France ; books are printed ; rebellions break
out against the Roman pontiffs ; traders and
sailors roam abroad ; Bacon reasons ; Shakespeare dramatizes ; the nation shuffles off the
coil of royal tyranny ; Royal Societies are
founded ; weavers weave ; spinners spin ;
bobbins and shuttles load ships ; chapter
succeeds chapter, till the great volume of
the nineteenth century is reached.

England has created the best and freest
government in the world ; England has made
the greatest literature ; England has brought
forth Bacon, Newton, Darwin ; England has
wrought the only system of law that can
match that of Rome ; England has sent forth

"comme un vol de gerfauts," adventurers,
colonizers, civilizers ; England, by Drake and
Howard of Effingham, has annexed the Channel to her coast ; England has sent westward
Raleigh and Cabot, Pilgrims to Massachu-
setts, younger sons to Virginia, Wolfe to
Canada, Clive and Warren Hastings to India, Dampier and Cook to Australia, Gordon
and Kitchener to Egypt, incorporating *vi
et armis* great regions of the earth to have
and to hold to her and her English heirs
forever.

Amid such prodigal wealth of harvest
there is room for many husbandmen. Hol-
inshed and Froissart may chronicle legend
and foray ; Bacon may find a narrative that
shall lead to political preferment ; Hakluyt
may gather yarns together that shall stop
the question, " What have the indolent English done at sea ? " Clarendon may prove the
badness of a fallen cause ; Hume may uncover plentiful proofs of Tory virtue ; Napier
may track the "thin red line of heroes"
threading the mountains of Spain. Out of
the hundred facets an historian may select
that one which flashes most light to him.
Froude may praise the red hands of Eliza-

bethan marauders; Gardiner may follow endless links of cause and effect; Freeman may
find explanations for his own historic doubts;
Lingard may gratify Roman Catholics; Green
may avoid personal prejudices. English history has great garners laden with probabilities, theories, interests, and facts, protean
enough to satisfy the most wanton historical
desires.

By the side of the gay and splendid colors
of English history, there are large quiet
spaces of sombre hues, dull to the indolent
eye. While heroes, paladins, and champions
have been caracoling conspicuous; sad-vis-
aged, shrewd, resolute men have been stead-
ily working, plodding, planning, construct-
ing, — commonly behind the scenes, but not
always. Men who gradually, step by step,
sadly and surely enlarging precedent, piecing
and patching, wrought the common law; who
slowly and steadfastly built up the pious and
sombre creeds and practices of the Nonconformist churches of England. Such men
have had a great and controlling influence
on the development of modern England.
They have been the burghers as opposed to
landowners or yeomen; of the middle class

as against the aristocracy and the plebeians ;
the educated in distinction from the learned
or the ignorant. They have been the dissenters and low churchmen ; they have been
the party of advance, the advocates of petty
changes, the practical men busy with daily
needs, careless of sentiments and theories,
taking care of the pennies of life.

They are the men of double entry, magni-
fying routine. In business they have added
mechanical device to mechanical device ; they
have put wind, water, steam, and electricity
into subjection ; they have done most of the
reckoning in England, and their brains are
hieroglyphed with *l. s. d.* They have built
up cities, adding house to house, block to
block, factory to factory; they also have
made a man's house his castle. The magic
of science does not affect them. It is a monster, a Caliban, for its usefulness they would
not heed it, —

> " But, as 't is,
> We cannot miss him : he does make our fire,
> Fetch in our wood, and serves in offices
> That profit us. What ho ! slave ! "

In literature they have sustained the names
that have been forgotten ; of art they are in-

nocent; in religion they are for the Old Testament; in English politics they are Whigs
and Liberals. They made the revolution of
1688; they passed the Act of Settlement, —
a formal declaration of an accepted principle
that no king had divine rights in Great Britain; they maintained the House of Hanover.

This cautious, industrious, peering-round-
the-corner class is not attractive to everybody.
We miss the glitter and the purple of ostentatious heroism; we feel the absence of luxury, of recklessness, of epigram, of *sangfroid*.
Nevertheless, that class constitutes most of
the machinery of the civilized world, calling
itself the party of progress, known to its
enemies as Mr. Gradgrind, Mr. Worldly-wise,
Mr. Stay-at-home. This difference between
the manufacturer and the country squire, the
artisan and the soldier, the practical man
and the idealist, an eye fixed on the present
and an eye roaming over the past or future,
between Whig and Tory, is the line of de-
marcation between two kinds of minds: the
Benjamin Franklin character, inclined to wise
saws, wise doubts, wise practices and experi-
ments; and the Dr. Johnson temperament,
bowing to authority, custom, the ways of

grandfathers, the traditions of grandmothers, full of crotchets, prejudices, beliefs, and idealism.

If one looks at these classes from the point of view of the reader on winter evenings, the attractions of Tory history (to use the political epithet), English conquests, English empire, English traditions, English poetry, are beyond comparison more entertaining than histories of the common law, of Presbyterian synods, of factory acts, of Manchesters and Birminghams. But when the world is quiet and the politics of England can regulate themselves by private morality and by the maxims of Poor Richard's Almanac, the outwardly uninteresting class is sure to be in power. The great wealth of England, the moral tone of her literature, the humane standard among her common clergy, the saving ballast in her ship of state, are all triumphs of the Whigs.

Two generations ago the chief historians of England, Clarendon, Hume, Lingard, had done little justice to the achievements of utility and progress; it was time that an advocate should arise to show the real value of the work of the middle classes. Justice

demanded that at the bar of public opinion a
zealous believer should plead the cause of the
Whigs.   Up rose Thomas Babington Macaulay, and first in the " Edinburgh Review,"
and afterwards in his History, eulogized
their political achievements with amazing eloquence.   All that he has written on the subject has been a splendid repetition of his words
on his election as member. for Edinburgh :
"I look with pride on all that the Whigs
have done for the cause of human freedom
and of human happiness."

II

As a political party, during Macaulay's
boyhood and early youth, the Whigs were at
a low point of their power. The horrors of
the Reign of Terror in Paris, the gigantic
attempt of Napoleon to subdue the world, the
obvious necessity of war, the glories of the
Nile, Trafalgar, of Torres Vedras and Waterloo, had kept the majority of Englishmen
in the Tory ranks. But after Napoleon had
been caged in St. Helena ; after the Holy
Alliance had guaranteed the peace of Europe ; after the change from war to peace had
thrown business into confusion, the minds

of Englishmen were free to meditate on the
defects of the time. The law, especially in
the Court of Chancery, dragged itself along
in loops of unjust delay; the criminal law
was barbarously severe; slavery still prevailed
in England's colonies; the slave trade had
but lately been suppressed; Roman Catholics
were disfranchised; the Church had fallen
into the hands of ignorant parsons; the House
of Commons was in the power of nobles and
great landowners. But the tide was turning. The Tories were losing their bulwark
of French fears; Lord Eldon and the Duke
of Wellington were growing old; while to the
support of the Whigs came the great force
of the early nineteenth century. Machinery
was developing Leeds, Manchester, and Birmingham; machinery was doubling their population and influence; machinery was making manufacturers rich, urging them to power
and freedom from old restraints. Weaving
and spinning were forcing the landed interests into matters of secondary importance.
The factories of England were calling to Glasgow, Liverpool, and London to cover the sea
with English ships; and English commerce
answered to the call. Behind machinery

stood the great genie steam, of pure Whig
principles, practical, energetic, heedless of the
past, eager for new things.

For a long time the opposition to old customs, habits of mind, ways of thought and
action had needed a mouthpiece. Believers
in change, advocates of novelty, critics of
what is and has been, stood in need of a
standard-bearer, especially in Scotland, where
the rising genius of Walter Scott was pran-
cing like "proud Cumberland." The spirit
of revolt was ready for articulate voice.
About the time when Macaulay was born,
Sydney Smith, Francis Jeffrey, Francis Horner, and Henry Brougham met in their " gar-
ret " in Edinburgh, and founded the " Edinburgh Review." That review now is part of
old political and literary history. The lives
of its founders have been written, their essays
have been collected, and the modern reader
ignorant of foes who have been long since
killed and buried, when he sees these doughty
champions belaboring thin air, wonders why
the founders of the " Edinburgh Review " are
still remembered. The youngest of them
and the most remarkable was Brougham.
He contributed many articles to the early

numbers, and continued to write for it throughout his life ; he wrote in all as many as two hundred essays.

Brougham was a man of enormous activity, an agitator, attacking with voice and pen hundreds of abuses with perpetual vigor and audacity. He worked with Wilberforce and Lord Holland against slavery and the slave trade. He assailed the Orders in Council, the Income Tax, the foes of Queen Caroline, the enemies of law reform. He fought for the diffusion of education. He argued, harangued, and debated in Parliament with the vigor of ten. He led the bar on the Northern circuit. He thundered against Lord Eldon day and night. He discoursed before reforming societies. He lectured to leagues for the promotion of scientific knowledge. Brougham became one of the most famous men in the House of Commons, and after the Whig triumph, when Lord Grey came into power in 1830, he was given the Great Seal. Such a powerful turbulent spirit exerted great influence on the Review. He disliked Macaulay, — out of jealousy, as Macaulay thought, — and when Jeffrey resigned his position as editor, Brougham

threw his weight against the proposal that
Macaulay should succeed him.

Sydney Smith was the oldest of the
founders, and a far more typical Whig than
Brougham. He was the embodiment of the
qualities which give its character to the English Church. Better than any history, Sydney Smith sets forth the practical morality,
the subordination of religion to the business
of living, the intolerance of mysticism, the
high esteem of common sense, which distin-
guishes the English Church. Sydney Smith
was a good man, an excellent parson, a
shrewd preacher. He looked on life from
the standpoint of common sense; he was interested in practical results. He thought
that the problems of government, of religion, of living, were all to be solved by intelligence and patience. He brought his wit
to the service of the liberal cause, and was
perhaps the most effective contributor to the
Review before Macaulay.

Francis Horner is generally forgotten. He
was a man of hard integrity and of studious
mind, with a leaning to metaphysics, eco-
nomics, and other studies then specially cultivated in Edinburgh. Sydney Smith said

that he had the Ten Commandments written
on his face. Horner died before he was
forty, cutting short a career in the House of
Commons that was assured of distinguished
success.

Francis Jeffrey was the controlling influence in this group of men. He guided and
governed. He selected and sifted; he kept
on good terms with the fiery Brougham.
He looked on the Review as a factor in civilization, and, it seems, hesitated to make it
a purely party organ. But Walter Scott and
Tory friends started the Quarterly in 1809,
and the "Edinburgh Review" thereupon became identified with the Whig political party.
Jeffrey must have been a very attractive
man; Sydney Smith was very fond of him;
Brougham remained faithful to him; Scott
speaks affectionately of him. He was most
kind to Macaulay. In his old age Macaulay's success with the "History of England"
delighted him: "My dear Macaulay, the
mother that bore you, had she been yet
alive, could scarcely have felt prouder or
happier than I do at this outburst of your
graver fame." Jeffrey's essays have become things of the past. The cold Words-

worthian, in his less worthy moods, looks up
the famous sentences of blame once so much
applauded. The opinions of literary men,
unless they chance to catch what succeeding
generations hold to be truth, or have dinted
their personality on their sentences, pass with
the harvests of last year. Macaulay gives
Jeffrey most generous praise, but Macaulay
spoke from a grateful heart.

In 1825 Jeffrey, not aware of all the forces
that were working on the Whig side, was
eagerly seeking young men of talents, when
he came upon a man of twenty-four, of fluent
speech, of prodigious memory and information, and untrammeled by a single doubt.
Young Macaulay contributed to the August
number his essay on Milton.

III

The Macaulays were Scotch. An anecdote
of Lord Macaulay's grandfather, who was one
of the ministers at Inverary when Dr. Johnson went thither on his trip to the Hebrides,
is told by Boswell, which gives an intima-
tion that in the Macaulay blood there was
both that readiness to block out a man's
character and make it all of a piece, and

that lack of sensitive imagination, of which
we find strong marks in the " History of
England." " When Dr. Johnson spoke of
people whose principles were good, but whose
practice was faulty, Mr. M'Aulay said, he had
no notion of people being in earnest in their
good professions whose practice was not suit-
able to them.   The Doctor grew warm, and
said, ' Sir, are you so grossly ignorant of human nature, as not to know that a man may
be very sincere in good principles, without
having good practice ? ' "   This is characteristic Tory criticism of characteristic Whig
belief.

This minister's son Zachary was of the
Scotch Puritan type.   Early bred to business he went at sixteen to Jamaica, where
he learned to hate negro slavery ; he gave
up his position in consequence, went back
to England at about twenty-four years of
age, and was sent out to Sierra Leone by a
company formed in the interest of liberated
slaves.   There he remained as governor of the
colony till 1799, when he returned to England and married a Miss Mills, the daughter
of a Quaker of Bristol.   On October 25, 1800,
Thomas Babington Macaulay was born.

One of Macaulay's many bits of good fortune has been his biographer; Trevelyan is unsurpassed by any Englishman except Boswell. In the "Life and Letters of Lord Macaulay," the precocious boy, the brilliant young man, appears in a holiday dress of delightful anecdotes. In that wonderful youth it is difficult to tell what effect Macaulay's father and mother had upon him. His father served the anti-slavery cause, in company of Wilberforce and Thornton, with stern and tireless devotion. He appears to have looked on his son somewhat as a means which God had given him for the execution of a great plan; not that there was any lack of affection, but the son never could have had the pleasure of beholding in his father a purpose to secure for him the fullness of life, never could have realized except in imagination that a father might bestow upon his son the education of mere prodigal love. Macaulay's mother was a devout woman, somewhat given to that pious phraseology which is tolerable only in privacy. There is a picture of evangelical Clapham — that part of London where the Macaulays lived — in "The Newcomes." Colonel Newcome's

father lived there; his brothers Hobson and
Brian were bred there. But Trevelyan will
not grant much truth to this picture.

After preparation at a small school Macaulay went into residence at Trinity College,
Cambridge, in October, 1818. Derwent Coleridge, Praed, and a certain brilliant Charles
Austin were among his intimates. Although
already a great reader, Macaulay did not live
in books only; he took keen interest in politics, wrote prize poems, talked early and late.
He had no liking for mathematics, for science, or for athletic exercises. He seems to
have been at that time very much what he
was in later years; with the same zeal, the
same quick spirit, and with those prodigious
powers of reading and of remembering, of
which the like have never been known. In
1822 he won the prize for the best essay on
the "Conduct and Character of William III."
Trevelyan says that the characters of James
and of William, the Popish Plot, the license
of the Restoration, " are drawn on the same
lines and painted in the same colors" as they
are in his History. This is characteristic of
the man. Macaulay lacked the advantage
of slowness in intellectual development, which

enables a growing mind to feed upon fitting
food in the advancing stages of its development. His capacity for sympathy seems to
have been of a certain quality, receptive
only within definite limits ; it had no elasti-
city to admit new classes of interests. His
enormous fund of information did him a
certain injury by coddling, as it were, the
stunted side of his imagination. It assured
him that his judgment had not been taken
without a complete survey of all reasonably
available means of knowledge. It lent all
the weight of precocious erudition to opinions formed too easily, and shut him off
from the elementary truth that not information, but sensitiveness to many sides of humanity, helps a man to just judgments. His
views were clear, definite, susceptible of support from many arguments, and honest as
the day ; but he never had the education of
a great private personal emotion. He never
was in love ; he never comprehended the
meaning of religion. Untouched by these
two great causes of human growth, Macaulay
left Cambridge a very efficient machine, self-
possessed, ready, eloquent, of high principle,
careless of vulgar success, with certain pecu-

liar powers of mind which in their order
have not been surpassed if they have ever
been equalled.

Macaulay was called to the bar in 1826;
he went on the Northern circuit, where he
met Brougham, but it seems that he had little or no practice. His inclination lay in
other directions; he displayed his oratory
before various societies, and his literary talents in " Knight's Quarterly Magazine." In
1825 his essay on Milton had been published
in the " Edinburgh Review," and he was at
once treated by notable men of twice his age
with distinguished consideration. Perhaps
it was a misfortune for a brilliant young
man of Scotch ancestry, bred at home in an
evangelical, anti-slavery air, trained to complete self-possession at Cambridge, to find
himself of instant consequence to the great
Whig organ. He was thereby subjected to
influences which strengthened his tenden-
cies of mind and cut him off from all sympathy with opposite opinions; so that the
very virtues of conservatism, of unreasoning
emotions, stood over against him as so many
enemies to be battled with.

Petted and praised by the men whom he

had learned to look upon as the salt of England, sought after by that Review for which
Sydney Smith, the great wit, Jeffrey, the
great critic, Brougham, the great reformer,
were eager to write, applauded by the whole
reading world of London, Macaulay had no
chance to repair the defects of his inheritance and of his education. The essay on
Milton is not one of Macaulay's best, — he
was but twenty-four years old, — yet it bears
the well-known characteristics of Macaulay's
style : clearness with no shadow of doubt;
the assurance that only a little patience and
common sense are needed, and all the confusion that time, custom, and prejudice have
thrown around the important matters of life
will uncurl and drop off, leaving one face to
face with certainty ; the brilliant mastery of
rhetoric which satisfies the immediate appe-
tite of the mind ; the powerful arguments
of the orator which upon one hearing are
not to be resisted ; the positiveness of common sense, the definiteness of complete comprehension, the art of prologue and exor-
dium, of paragraph and sentence, of commas
and semicolons. All his life Macaulay was
convinced that truth is as clear as day, and

that if a man has knowledge of his subject and is neither a bigot nor a fool, he need only write clearly and all people past rudimentary intelligence and shell-form education will receive light and be converted. He felt the burden of Whig duty upon his shoulders; he must show the right and describe the wrong, portray justice and reveal injustice, exhibit the beneficial and expose the hurtful, put the light of good literature on a hill and snuff the candle of the bad. Macaulay had the highest aims and the noblest aspirations that are compatible with complete mental subjection to the practical, to the useful, to the mechanical parts of life. He is intolerant of wrong, because wrong is his adversary, and his adversary is wrong. He hates injustice; has not injustice been ranged with Stuarts, pretenders, slavery, Popery, and all the evils he is resolute to combat? He abhors cruelty; it is inextricably bound up with bigotry, fanatical loyalty, intolerant privileges. He is a man of party; he enjoys friends, he delights in enemies. He rejoices in his own strength, and hits out from the shoulder.

He who looks back over two generations

at the fierce battles of the past finds it easy
to see virtue and wrong on each side, discovers the vanity of the victory and the hol-
lowness of the defeat, and in his armchair,
turning over books, smiles at the fiery zeal and
convictions of men long buried. None the
less is it important for him that the battle
has been fought, that the side on which there
was a slight preponderance of right should
have conquered. We may wonder at the
emotions of those who fought the political
fight over the Reform Act, with somewhat of
the same compassion that we read of Atha-
nasian and Arian, but we need to remember
that not the indolent skepticisms of the past,
but its vigorous energies and convictions,
have removed stones and uprooted thorns
from our path.

IV

The great struggle between the old political institutions of England and the new
political needs of the middle classes was first
fought over the question of Roman Catholic
Emancipation. The reformers won. The
Test Acts were old statutes enacted in the
time of Charles II., and required all officers,

civil and military, under the government to
take the communion according to the rites
of the Anglican Church. Thereafter those
Acts had been in substance amended by
allowing dissenters to be relieved from the
penalties of the original Acts, but they had
remained in full force against the Catholics.
These Acts were repealed in 1828. In 1829
the Catholic Emancipation Act, which allowed Roman Catholics to sit in Parliament,
was passed. Both parties then prepared for
the great issue of parliamentary reform.

At that time the House of Commons did
not represent the nation but the aristocracy.
Great landowners sent their sons and depend-
ents to sit for pocket boroughs. Members
sat for constituencies which had been established hundreds of years and more; in the
mean time some old towns had dwindled to
villages. Old Sarum had no inhabitants,
yet it returned two members. Old villages
had grown to great cities, and had no representation. Manchester, Leeds, Birmingham,
Sheffield, returned no members; Edinburgh,
Glasgow, London itself, were most imper-
fectly represented. The House represented
neither population nor property. The pros-

perous middle classes throughout the whole
island determined that this injustice should
cease, that they should share with the aristocracy. The Whigs were on the lookout for
young men of talents. In the early part of
1830, through the influence of Lord Lans-
downe, Macaulay was returned to Parliament for a petty borough. In July George
IV. died, and Parliament was dissolved. The
new elections were held on the issue of parliamentary reform; the Whigs were successful. Shortly after Parliament assembled the
Duke of Wellington was forced to resign,
and Earl Grey formed a Whig ministry.
Brougham was made lord chancellor. On
the first day of March, 1831, Lord John
Russell, leader in the House, introduced the
Reform Bill, which proposed to disfranchise
some threescore boroughs, and to give representation to unrepresented towns. The next
day Macaulay, who had addressed the House
but twice in the preceding Parliament, arose
and delivered his first great speech. He
said that the bill was a practical measure,
that it did not propose to embody a symmet-
rical theory of representation; he would not
urge universal suffrage for fear lest in times

of discontent the laboring classes should be wrought upon by passion to do hurt to the state; but this bill would bring great strength of property and intelligence to the support of order. He argued that to say the present system was ancient, and in old times had been praised by Englishmen and foreigners, was no defense of it; in those times there had been a representative House of Commons, but great changes in population and property had taken place; that the Tory argument that Manchester was virtually represented was a concession to reform, for if virtual representation was good, in what respect was it good wherein direct representation would not be better; that, to the fear that the middle classes were desirous of abolishing the monarchy and the aristocracy, he would answer that a form of government in which the middle classes had no confidence could not conduce to the happiness of the people; that, as to the claim that it would be unjust to deprive boroughs of vested rights, history showed that the right to return members had never been regarded as property; that change was better than discontent. Did the House wish to wait for popular rage? "Now, therefore, while everything at home and abroad forebodes ruin to those who persist in a hopeless struggle against the spirit of the age, now, while the crash of the proudest throne of the Continent is still resounding in our ears, now, while the roof of a British palace affords an ignominious shelter to the exiled heir of forty kings, now, while we see on every side ancient institutions subverted, and great societies dissolved, now, while the heart of England is still sound, now, while old feelings and old associations retain a power and a charm which may too soon pass away, now, in this your accepted time, now, in this your day of salvation, take counsel, not of prejudice, not of party spirit, not of the ignominious pride of a fatal consistency, but of history, of reason, of the ages which are past, of the signs of this most portentous time. Renew the youth of the state. Save property divided against itself. Save the multitude endangered by its own ungovernable passions. Save the aristocracy, endangered by its own unpopular power. Save the greatest, and fairest, and most highly civilized community that ever existed, from calamities which may in a few days

sweep away all the rich heritage of so many
ages of wisdom and glory. The danger is
terrible. The time is short." The House
was wild with excitement. Everybody compared him to Burke, Fox, Canning. Peel
said that parts of the speech were as beautiful as anything he had ever heard or read.
Macaulay, the orator, had rivaled Macaulay
of the " Edinburgh Review." Society ran
after him. Rogers gave him breakfast parties ; Lady Holland made a pet of him.
Gladstone says that Macaulay had achieved
" immense distinction." " For a century and
more, perhaps no man in this country, with
the exception of Mr. Pitt and Lord Byron,
had attained at thirty-two the fame of Macaulay. His parliamentary success and his
literary eminence were each of them enough,
as they stood at this date, to intoxicate any
brain and heart of a meaner order. But to
these was added in his case an amount and
quality of social attentions such as invaria-
bly partake of adulation and idolatry, and
as perhaps the high circles of London never
before or since have lavished on a man whose
claims lay only in himself, and not in his
descent, his rank, or his possessions." Never-

theless, Macaulay devoted himself to Parliament. In the autumn the House of Lords threw out the bill. The country was very much excited. The Commons passed the bill again, the Lords indicated that their minds were unchanged. Earl Grey resigned. The Duke of Wellington tried to form a cabinet, but could not, and advised the king to recall the Whig ministry. The threat of creating new peers sufficient to turn the Lords to a Whig body was successful. The bill passed, and on the 7th of June, 1832, became law.

The victory was much to the honor of England. By the force of public opinion expressed in the forms of law the fabric of the British constitution had been greatly changed. The chief of the coördinate branches of the government had been taken out of the hands of the aristocracy and given to the middle classes. Englishmen had effected this revolution by peaceful methods. No blood was shed, no soldiers paraded the streets, neither legal rights nor ordinary business was suspended; while on the Continent in Germany, France, Italy, Belgium, and Poland, reformers and conservatives had been shooting one another in the highways.

These important events left their mark on Macaulay; the natural bent of his shrewd practical mind was increased and strengthened. He had deepened his likings and broadened his dislikes. He saw all English history explained and interpreted by this parliamentary struggle. When his mind again went to the subject of his prize essay, he felt that the country had been through a revolution like that of 1688; and that his personal experience enabled him to understand James II. and William III. as no man who had not been in the middle of that struggle could do. It is no wonder that a young man of strong feelings, who had borne an honorable part in the contest, and had won a great reputation, should have become more and more convinced that the dividing line between Whig and Tory was the very line which separated right from wrong; and that when he looked back over the history of England, he should have judged the past by the present.

V

Macaulay's collected essays fill several volumes. All but a few were published in the

"Edinburgh Review" from 1825 to 1845.
Of his first essay, that on Milton, he himself
says it "contains scarcely a paragraph such
as my matured judgment approves, and is
overloaded with gaudy and ungraceful ornament." Howbeit, a gay livery becomes the
opinions of youth. The essay on Milton is
boyish, not with the ordinary immaturity of
four and twenty, but with the boyishness of
Macaulay's own schoolboy of twelve; he who
at fifteen in the Seminary of Douai learned
enough theology to outweigh the Jesuit
counselors of Charles II. and James II., and
whose private library would be incomplete
without a full edition of Burnet's pamphlets.
Nevertheless, of all blame laid on Charles I.,
most people best remember the famous sum-
ming up: "We charge him with having
broken his coronation oath; and we are told
that he kept his marriage vow." The essay
is boyish, but fifty years after it was published, Mr. Gladstone, at the age of sixty-
five, deemed it worthy of criticism.

In the essays many little mistakes of fact
have been discovered by careful seekers.
Froude charges Macaulay with error upon
error: in that Macaulay makes accusation

that Alice Perrers was mistress of Edward III., that Strafford debauched the daughter of Sir Richard Bolton, that Henry VIII. was the murderer of his wives. Froude's pleas of not guilty savor a little of the technical knowledge of an advocate at the criminal bar retained for the defense. Macaulay's statements may technically not be proved; as jurymen we may say not guilty, but as individuals we are convinced of the justice of his charge. Froude, champion of the Protestant cause, accuses Macaulay of wrong to the English Reformation and to Cranmer; and of espousal of the Catholic cause in 1829; but betrays his own intemperate partiality by adding: "The Ethiopian, it was said, had changed his skin." Froude also finds fault that Macaulay was too severe in his essay on Robert Montgomery's bad poems. What place has generosity in matters of art?

Froude says Macaulay "was the creation and representative of his own age; what his own age said and felt, whether it was wise or foolish, Macaulay said and felt." In this judgment Mr. John Morley and Mr. Leslie Stephen concur. It may be that to be the representative of the age is no very serious fault. Shakespeare bears witness to the high renaissance of England; Dante embodies the Middle Ages; Cervantes represents the chivalry of Spain; Abraham Lincoln is the flower of American democracy. Macaulay, it is true, never tires telling of the growth of population and the increase of wealth; and many men whose minds, like his, are, as Froude says, "of an ordinary kind," think exactly as he does. But their creed is the creed of England. Is it surely wrong? Perhaps we should rejoice at the increase of wisdom and not at multiplying numbers; but what of an hundred thousand mothers who rejoice over an hundred thousand children? Whose newborn son shall be handed to Herod as the price of wisdom? And what becomes of the sneer at commercial prosperity when we think of food for the hungry, shelter for the ragged, schools for the ignorant, homes for the aged? It is not the beliefs, but the skepticisms of the utilitarian which are to be blamed.

It may be asked, is Froude's fame the triumph of accuracy? is Mr. Morley wholly free from the popular positivist creed of his generation? has he in "Voltaire" and "Rousseau" betrayed sympathy with an alien faith? Is

Mr. Leslie Stephen in danger lest he be flung from the saddle of common sense by the caracoling of his rhetoric? They all complain that Macaulay lacks sensitiveness. The complaint is just; but are they in a position to claim that their own title to distinction is " d'avoir quelquefois pleuré "?

Macaulay's essays taken one by one can be splintered and chipped, but bound together they furnish part of the strength of English literature. Their subjects have great range of historical interest; vast knowledge of literature has been crammed into their compass; mastery of rhetoric colors page, paragraph, and sentence. Picture follows picture till the reader fancies that he is whirled by spring floods from Shalott castle down to many towered Camelot. Like a genie to the lord of his lamp, Macaulay fetches the wealth of all the literature of the civilized world and lays it before his readers. He goes through a volume for an anecdote; he ransacks a library for an impression.

There is one danger into which Macaulay's critics often fall. In the picture of a man, in the narration of an episode, they find an error of fact, and conclude that the picture

is unjust, that the episode is false. But
Macaulay is so steeped in information that,
although he may be wrong as to a particular
fact, he is justified in his conclusion. In the
case of Henry VIII. there may be legal error
and moral truth in the epithet murderer.

The essays are the work of a rhetorician,
the greatest, perhaps, in English literature.
One defect in that literature, as compared with
Latin literatures, has been a lack of rhetoric.
The great masters of English prose, Milton
and Burke, appeal to the imagination. Their
language is sensuous and adorned, but they
address themselves to the intellect; they
charge their speech with thought; they are
careless that they lay burdens upon their readers; they are indifferent that they outstride
the crowd. The rhetorician — a Cicero, a
Bossuet — tries to spare his readers; he
wishes to be always thronged by the multitude. So it is with Macaulay. He says
nothing that everybody cannot comprehend
and at once. He exerts all his powers to
give his readers as little to do as possible;
he drains his memory to find decorations to
catch their eye and fix their attention. He
presents everything in brilliant images. He

writes to the eye and the ear. He has in mind the ordinary Briton ; he does not write for a sect nor for a band of disciples. He is always the orator talking to men who are going to vote at the close of his speech. He never stops with a suggestion ; he never pauses with a hint ; he is never tentative, never is rendered august by the clouds of doubt.

Macaulay was a born orator fit to speak to the multitude at the cross-roads ; not to the individual in his closet : he was also a man of letters, a man of the library ; no living being ever had such a mass of information in his head at one time. These two qualities explain his devotion to literature, his admiration of the Greeks, his love of the world's great poets, and the seemingly inconsistent fact that he never exceeded the stature of a rhetorician. He had a skilled, delicate, and educated taste in literature ; but his ear to listen and his voice to speak were far apart. His ear is the cunning ear of Jacob listening to the sweet voice of Rachel, but his voice is the voice of Esau calling afar to his shepherds.

Macaulay's poetry is himself set to metre

and rhyme. It has the swing, the vigor, the
balanced sentences of his prose. It has the
awakening power of brass instruments playing the reveille. It used to be a subject
of debate whether Macaulay's poems were
poetry or no ; and there are men to whom
those poems have not and never can have
the significance of the poetry native to them.
But they are the poetry of a strong, healthy,
typical Englishman. It may be doubted if
there be any other English poetry which
bears in itself half so much evidence that it
was written by an Englishman. The metre
is good, the rhyme is good, the narrative is
excellent. Everybody knows how the strenu-
ous rush of Horatius dints itself on the memory ; everybody can name the cities which
sent their tale of men to Lars Porsena.

Macaulay in his verse as in his prose presents one definite picture after another. Each
character comes on the stage in exact portraiture, whether it be Horatius, Herminius,
Halifax, Sunderland, or Somers. There they
are in the blaze of high noon ; there is no
twilight for them ; never do their outlines
blend in the shades of doubt. Macaulay saw
the world as one vast picture-book. This

is the reason why his essays stand on the
Australian's shelf next to the Bible and to
Shakespeare. There is nothing in English
literature comparable to them ; there is nothing of the kind in foreign literatures.
Each essay is a combination of history and
literature, of anecdote and learning, of incident and portraiture, of advocacy and party
spirit, such as are commonly found separate
and distinct in the essays of a dozen different men. There is somewhat of the con-
structive element of imagination here. As
the mechanical mind brings together the
odds and ends of its recollection, the remainder baggage of its memory, and works
and fashions them into an invention, so
Macaulay from his vast stores unites and
combines scattered materials and creates an
imaginative picture. There is nothing to be
found in his work which the world did not
possess before; but most of the world was
not aware of its possessions until Macaulay
gathered them together.

VI

Next in importance to Macaulay's experience in Parliament, as bearing upon his

historical education, are his four years of
service in India. One of the early acts of
the Reformed Parliament was to revise the
charter of the East India Company. Among
great changes it was enacted that one member of the Supreme Council, which, with
the governor-general, was to govern India,
should not be chosen from the service of the
company. Macaulay was appointed to fill
that position, and in 1834, taking his sister
Hannah, subsequently Lady Trevelyan, he
sailed for India. To the general reader the
most interesting event connected with Macaulay's service in India is a list of the books
he read on the voyages thither and back.
On the voyage out, he read the Iliad, the
Odyssey, the Æneid, Horace, Cæsar, Bacon,
Dante, Petrarch, Ariosto, Tasso, Cervantes,
"The Decline and Fall of Rome," Mill's
"India," seventy volumes of Voltaire, Sis-
mondi's "History of France," and the seven
folios of the "Biographica Britannica." The
real matters of consequence are Macaulay's
study of the details of Indian administration, his support of complete freedom of the
press, his successful advocacy that all the
higher branches of knowledge should be

taught in the English tongue; and, more than all, his labors upon the Criminal Code. Of his draft of this Code after spending great and continuous labor upon it, Macaulay says: " I am not ashamed to acknowledge that there are several chapters in the Code on which I have been employed for months; of which I have changed the whole plan ten or twelve times; which contain not a single word as it originally stood; and with which I am very far indeed from being satisfied." After Macaulay's return to England, in 1838, his draft was revised by a successor, and was finally enacted into law after the Mutiny.

In those four years Macaulay took a large share in the administration of an empire; while tending its needs he observed the operations of social forces which when past constitute the history of a country. In his leisure time he read books as no man ever read before. When he returned to England he had had the worst and the best training for writing history that ever an Englishman had: in that he had been a partisan legislator at a time when the enactment of a British statute was the formal

acknowledgment of a social revolution; and
in that he had been administrator of the empire of India in a time of transition. These
experiences gave him an intimate knowledge
of the machinery of government; but sometimes in matters of history the hand of little
employment hath the daintier sense. When
we consider that in addition to this education
he had a marvelous power of expression, a
prodigious memory, and an interest in English history greater than in anything else,
it might have been guessed that Macaulay
would write the most brilliant history of
England that had yet been written.

On July 20, 1838, Macaulay, writing to
Napier, editor of the " Edinburgh Review,"
of his proposed History, said that according
to his plan it should extend from the Revolution to the death of George IV.; "the
history would then be an entire view of all
the transactions which took place between
the Revolution which brought the Crown
into harmony with the Parliament and the
Revolution which brought the Parliament
into harmony with the nation." On December 18 his diary reads: "I am more and
more in love with my subject. I really

think that posterity will not willingly let my book die." Nevertheless, it was long before he was able to give himself wholly to his task. In the summer of that year he was asked to stand for the city of Edinburgh. On his election he accepted the secretary-ship at war and a seat in Lord Melbourne's cabinet. The Whigs, however, were losing their hold upon the people, and in the general election in 1841, although Macaulay was returned again from Edinburgh, the Tories carried everything south of the Trent, and Macaulay lost his seat in the cabinet. He was glad of greater leisure, and went busily to work at essays, at his " Lays of Ancient Rome," and at his History.

Once again he sat in the cabinet. Sir Robert Peel was beaten in June, 1846, and Lord John Russell gave Macaulay a seat as paymaster-general of the army. But his term of office was again short, for he was defeated at the polls in the next general election in 1847.

Free from parliamentary duties Macaulay worked at his History with unimpeded industry; he devoured books, pamphlets, manuscripts, papers, letters; he traveled hither

and thither, to this place and to that; he
followed lines of march, he traced marks of
old walls and bastions, he ferreted out traditions, he listened to old gossip. "The notes
made during his fortnight's tour through
the scenes of the Irish war are equal in
bulk to a first-class article in the Edinburgh
or Quarterly reviews." The first two volumes of the History appeared in November,
1848. Success was instantaneous. Macaulay had said : "I shall not be satisfied unless
I produce something which shall for a few
days supersede the last fashionable novel on
the tables of young ladies." He must have
been satisfied. Edition has succeeded edition, paid for and pirated, in England, in
America, in a dozen foreign countries, volumes upon volumes, until it may be doubted
if any book, except the Bible, has had so
many copies printed. In December, 1855,
the third and fourth volumes were published; and Macaulay's fame as one of the
great English writers of the nineteenth century was firmly fixed in English literature.
"All the world wondered;" most of the
world applauded. Yet on the day when his
first volumes came out he writes in his diary :

"I read my book, and Thucydides, which, I am sorry to say, I found much better than mine." In comparison with any other rivals he felt content; and as he was free from petty vanity, his opinion is entitled to respect. In heaped masses of detail, in brilliant narrative, in clearness of meaning, in striking portraiture, in the portrayal of the chief characteristics of the English character, Macaulay has no English rival.

VII

It would be easy to find fault with any story of past events, even if it were written by Minos and Rhadamanthus together. The historian must tell in a chapter the events of years; he must compress into a page the character of a hero; he must cram into a paragraph an episode which brought life or death to a thousand men. With innumerable facts to choose from, he is bound to make choice. By the law of individuality he will not choose just the facts that Tom, Dick, or Harry sets store by. That Stubbs, Freeman, Hallam, Gardiner, do not have as many fault-finders as Macaulay is due in a measure, at least, to the fact that they have not one

fiftieth part of his readers; and the readers
whom they have belong to certain general
classes. Macaulay's readers are of every
kind and description : of crabbed age and
fiery youth; grave seniors, reckless ne'er-do-
wells; obstinate men, reasonable men; chol-
eric men, meek men; pinched men, pampered
men; misers, prodigals; saints, sinners; cyn-
ics, believers; the melancholy man, the curious man, the mean man, the envious man, —
all kinds from Brabantio to Autolycus, from
Major Pendennis to Mr. Winkle; and every
one a critic, caring not who knows his mind.

There are, however, several classes of men
to whom Macaulay's History wears an essentially false aspect. These are, first, the men
of Tory cast of thought, of whom we have
spoken: men who have been taught from
babyhood to look upon the cause represented
by Tories in the history of politics as the
only true and just cause; men who sit at
ease in the *status quo* and wonder why other
men squirm in their seats; men whose minds
clinging to the past, —

"Sois-moi fidèle, ô pauvre habit que j'aime !"

look askance at the future and possible

change; who face to-morrow in the posture of self-defense. They judge by local custom and immemorial usage, "My father used to say that his grandfather said," and cross themselves. Naturally they look upon the liberal type with an unjust eye.

In the second place, there are men of religious nature: men who give as little ear to daily happenings as they do to unknown tongues; who care not for the reputed meaning of things; who read Plato, Spinoza, Wordsworth; who roam about seeking something that shall satisfy their sense of bigness; who plunge into learning, bigotry, or sacrifice, as headlong as a boy dives into a summer pool. These men cannot take the Whig interpretation of life. Macaulay's facts are to them incoherent, meaningless; he might as well hold out to them a handful of sand. What are those gay faceted little facts to them? What care they for machinery, parliamentary reform, progress, Manchester prints? They delight not in gaudy day; they are servants to darkness, —

"Hail thou most sacred venerable thing."

Then there is a third class of men suscepti-

ble to delicate and indefinite sensations. They
demand chiaroscuro, twilight, " shadows and
sunny glimmerings." They are of a sensitive, skeptical quality. They hold that the
meaning of one solitary fact cannot be exhausted by the most brilliant description;
they must needs go back to it continually,
like Claude Monet to his haystack; every
time they find it different. They live in
mystery and uncertainty. The past is to
them as doubtful as the future. For them
some infinite spirit hovers over life, continually endowing it with its own attribute of
infinite change, forever wreathing this misty
matter into new shapes; making all things
uncommon, wonderful, and strange. For
them the highest of man's nature is in his
shudder of awe. For them all life has fitful
elements of poetry, music, and art. They
are sensitive to little things, moving about
like children in a world unrealized. They
are sympathetic with seeming mutually exclusive things. Such men seek poetry everywhere, and find it; they contemplate life as
an aggregate of possibilities, not of facts. At
common happenings, like opium-eaters, they
fall into strange dreams. They live on sym-

bols. To such an aspect of life as these men
behold, Macaulay was utterly strange. Of a
chapel in Marseilles he says : " The mass was
nearly over. I stayed to the end, wondering
that so many reasonable beings could come
together to see a man bow, drink, bow again,
wipe a cup, wrap up a napkin, spread his
arms, and gesticulate with his hands ; and to
hear a low muttering which they could not
understand, interrupted by the occasional
jingling of a bell."

Macaulay seems to have felt his estrange-
ment in a childlike way whenever he had to
do with those matters of beauty which peculiarly call out the distinctive character of
this class of men. " I have written several
things on historical, political, and moral
questions, of which, on the fullest recon-
sideration, I am not ashamed, and by which
I should be willing to be estimated; but I
have never written a page of criticism on
poetry, or the fine arts, which I would not
burn if I had the power." And yet Macaulay had strong feelings for two great ideal-
ists of the world, Dante and Cervantes. In
Florence his rooms looked out on a court
adorned with orange trees and marble stat-

ues.   His diary reads: "I never look at the
statues without thinking of poor Mignon:—

"'Und Marmorbilder stehn und sehn mich an :
Was hat man dir, du armes Kind, gethan ?'

I know no two lines in the world which I
would sooner have written than those."   In
another part of his diary he writes: "I
walked far into Herefordshire, and read,
while walking, the last five books of the
Iliad, with deep interest and many tears.   I
was afraid to be seen crying by the parties
of walkers that met me as I came back; crying for Achilles cutting off his hair, crying
for Priam rolling on the ground in the court-
yard of his house; mere imaginary beings,
creatures of an old ballad-maker who died
near three thousand years ago."   To such
sentiments few have been as susceptible as
Macaulay, but beyond that into the realm of
spiritual sensitiveness, into the borderland
where the senses cease to tyrannize, he could
not go.

Then there are men of individual idiosyn-
crasies: one does not like the popularity of
Macaulay's History, he prefers that which is
caviare to the general, a privacy of glorious
light must be his; a second is troubled by

antitheses and rhetoric; a third, hazy with
old saws, thinks that in so much glitter there
can be no gold; a fourth wants humor, he
misses the "tender blossoming" of Charles
Lamb here and there; others are Quakers
zealous for William Penn; doctors of philosophy tender of Bacon's good name; grand-
sons of Scotch cavaliers warm for Dundee;
militiamen valiant for Marlborough; then
there are Mr. Churchill Babington, Sir Francis Palgrave, and Gladstone himself, defend-
ers of the Anglican Church, and, not least,
Macaulay's fellow historians. How can a
just man please men of such varying hu-
mors? How shall a man write history for a
fellow scholar? How hold the balances between yesterday and to-morrow? How can
a man be neither for the party of change
nor for the party that says "tarry awhile."
"C'est une plaisante imagination de conce-
voir un esprit balancé justement entre deux
pareilles envyes."

Macaulay's History suits the majority of
Englishmen, by its virile directness, its honest clearness, its bold definiteness. Macaulay is never afraid; he never shirks, he never
dissembles or cloaks; he never says "per-

haps " or " maybe," nor " the facts are obscure," nor " authorities differ." He makes
the reader know just what effect the evidence
has produced on his mind. To be sure,
there is danger in that brilliant rhetoric.
The glow of declamation disdains the sickly
hue of circumspection. The reader of the
year 3000, for whom Macaulay winds his
horn, cannot hear the shuffling syllables of
shambling uncertainties. Men go to the
window when a fire engine gallops through
the street; a gentler summons might not
fetch them. There is something of martial
music about Macaulay's prose. There is that
in it which excites a man. It belongs to a
great advocate, not to blindfolded Justice
holding her cautious scales and doling out
" ifs," " buts," " howevers," as she balances
probabilities with all the diffidence of Doubt.
But what is truth? Shall Pilate tell of his
administration in Judæa? If he do, will it
be as definitive as the Koran in the eyes of
the Caliph Omar? Will Pilate leave the
Evangelists superfluous?

VIII

Macaulay was essentially, and in his strongest characteristics, an Englishman. His mind and heart were cast in English moulds. His great love and unbounded admiration of England sprung from his inner being. His morality, his honesty, his hate of sham, his carelessness of metaphysics, his frank speech, his insular understanding, his positiveness, are profoundly English. And there is in him something of that tenderness — to which in public he could give no adequate expression — which gives its grace to that most honorable epithet, an English gentleman. The real English gentleman shows his quality in his English home. Trevelyan has done as much for admiration of Macaulay, as oratory, essays, poetry, and history have, by giving us Macaulay's letters, and by telling us of Macaulay at home.

It would be a far cry to another man who has poured forth so much prodigal affection upon his sisters and their children. A Raleigh, a Bayard, do their famous acts of courtesy to sovereigns in presence of a court ; Macaulay did his acts of chivalry in secret.

With patience, pain, and tender solicitude,
he spent his splendid gifts for the pleasure
of simple women, and of boys and girls.
In his youth he was the delight of his sisters; in his manhood he was their pride,
their joy, and their benefactor. In all his
brilliant story, his letters to his sister Hannah, his little acts of kindness, his relations
to his nephews and nieces, are the most interesting passages.

In the midst of his triumph after his great
speech on the Reform Bill, he writes from
London : "My dear Sister, — I cannot tell
you how delighted I am to find that my letters amuse you. Send me some gossip, my
love. Tell me how you go on with German.
What novel have you commenced? or rather,
how many dozen have you finished? Re-
commend me one." While he was in India
he wrote, on the death of his youngest sister, "What she was to me no words can express. I will not say that she was dearer to
me than anything in the world, for my sister
who was with me was equally dear; but she
was as dear to me as one human being can
be to another." In a late diary he writes :
"Margaret, alas! alas! And yet she might

have changed to me. But no; that could
never have been. To think that she has
been near twenty-two years dead; and I am
crying for her as if it were yesterday."

He was a great playmate with Lady Trevelyan's little girls. He romped with them;
made poems for them, wrote them doggerel
verses and jolly letters. " Michaelmas will,
I hope, find us all at Clapham over a noble
goose. Do you remember the beautiful
Puseyite hymn on Michaelmas day? It is a
great favorite with all Tractarians. You and
Alice should learn it. It begins: —

> ' Though Quakers scowl, though Baptists howl,
>   Though Plymouth Brethren rage,
> We Churchmen gay will wallow to-day
>   In apple-sauce, onions, and sage.

> ' Ply knife and fork, and draw the cork,
>   And have the bottle handy;
> For each slice of goose will introduce
>   A thimbleful of brandy.'

Is it not good? I wonder who the author
can be. Not Newman, I think. It is above
him. Perhaps it is Bishop Wilberforce."
From his home at Holly Lodge at Kensing-
ton he writes to his youngest niece: " I have
had no friends near me but my books and

my flowers, and no enemies but those execrable dandelions. I thought that I was rid of the villains ; but the day before yesterday, when I got up and looked out of my window, I could see five or six of their great, impudent, flaring, yellow faces turned up at me. ' Only you wait till I come down,' I said. Is it Christian-like to hate a dandelion so savagely ? " He writes in his diary at Florence that he saw in the cloister at Santa Croce " a monument to a little baby, ' Il piu bel bambino che mai fosse ; ' not a very wise inscription for parents to put up, but it brought tears into my eyes. I thought of the little thing (a baby niece) who lies in the cemetery at Calcutta."

The end of his life was full of honors ; the city of Edinburgh returned him to Parliament unsolicited, eager to repair the wrong she had done in rejecting him ; Lord Palmerston's government made him a peer. In 1858 Motley writes : " It is always delightful to meet Macaulay, and to see the reverence with which he is regarded by everybody." He died on December 28, 1859. On Macaulay's tombstone in Westminster Abbey are the words : —

"His body lies buried in peace,
But his name liveth forever more."

And since Trevelyan's book not his name only, but the manner of man that he was. Of the very best type of Englishman, of the very straitest sect of Whigs in all except his brilliancy, there, in his biography he stands, in his courage, his convictions, his honesty, his nobility, his tenderness. Others may denounce shams and preach against affectation; Macaulay's whole life was one eulogy upon plain speech, one continued freedom from make-believe. He never was a pretender. In India, in the midst of awful beliefs, of strange ceremonies, of notions that lie outside our own humanity, where intensity of life is not admired, where force is incuriously regarded, where fame and honor are not the lessons of children, where chastity is not the pride of woman nor possessions the distinction of man, where sensuous flowers exhale perfumes that would wither up " wee modest " English flowers, Macaulay made no pretense of appreciation, but worked at a Criminal Code, and read European classics as if he were in Shropshire.

In Italy he is ready to burst into tears

when he has crossed the portal of St. Peter's;
but for him "nobody can think Saint Mark's
beautiful." He is shocked and disgusted by
"the monstrous absurdity of bringing doges,
archangels, cardinals, apostles, persons of the
Trinity, and members of the Council of Ten
into one composition."

In England all that Newman, Carlyle, Ruskin stood for, passed by him as unheeded as
a "threshold brook."

Macaulay's fame as a man of letters seems
as secure as that of any Englishman of this
century. Editions of the Essays and History
still come on. In Germany there are numerous translations. In France Taine has said:
"The great novelists penetrate the soul of
their characters, assume their feelings, ideas,
language. Such was Balzac. . . . With a
different talent Macaulay has the same power.
An incomparable advocate, he pleads an infinite number of causes; and he is master of
each cause, as fully as his client. Though
English, he had the spirit of harmony." In
Italy Professor Villari cites his opinion upon
Macchiavelli, delivered when he was twenty-
six, as of the greatest authority. In the
United States his books have been pirated,

and his style imitated. The generation of the year 2000 no doubt will read him. As to them of 3000, who cares? Many men greater than he are likely to be born, before another of such peculiar gifts who shall embody so brilliantly the best English characteristics.

ENGLISH AND FRENCH LITERATURE

ENGLISH AND FRENCH LITERATURE

I

THE French have had hospitable reception from us of late years; their books have been read with diligence, their novels have strewn ladies' tables, their ideas have inspired our men of letters. "Englished," "done into English," translated, converted, transfused into English, French literature furnishes forth our young ladies with conversation and our young gentlemen with cosmopolitanism, until the crushed worm of national prejudice begins to squirm and turn. Flaubert the high aspiring, Maupassant the cunning craftsman, Bourget the puppet-shifter, Zola the zealot, have had their innings; their side is out; the fiery bowling of Mr. Kipling has taken their last wicket, and those of us who have been born and bred in prejudice and provincialism may return to our English-American ways with a fair measure of jauntiness. We are no longer ashamed to lose

interest when we hear of an "inevitable"
catastrophe or of an "impeccable" style; we
yawn openly over " bitterly modern spiritual
complexities." Let us have done with raw
admiration of foreigners; let us no more
heed Ibsen and Zola,

" Or what the *Norse* intends, or what the French."

Let us speak out our prejudices; let us uncover our honest thoughts and our real affections. Let us openly like what nature has
commanded us to like, and not what we
should were we colossi spanning the chasm
between nations.

Cosmopolitanism spreads out its syllables
as if it were the royal city of humanity, but
if, whenever its praises are sung, the context
be regarded, the term is found to be only a
polysyllabic equivalent for Paris and things
Parisian; it means preference of French
ideas and ways to English. We are not
cosmopolitan; we learned our French history
from Shakespeare, Marryat, and Punch, and
from a like vantage-ground of literary simplicity we survey the courses of English and
French literatures, and with the definiteness
of the unskeptical we believe that in novel

and story, in drama and epic, in sermon and essay, in ballad and song, the English have overmatched the French.

The heart of all literature is poetry. The vitality of play, story, sermon, essay, of whatever there is best in prose, is the poetic essence in it. English prose is better than French prose, because of the poetry in it. We do not mean prose as a vehicle for useful information, but prose put to use in literature. English prose gets emotional capacity from English poetry, not only from the spirit of it, but also by adopting its words. English prose has thus a great poetical vocabulary open to it, and a large and generous freedom from conventional grammar. It draws its nourishment from English blank verse, and thus strengthened strides onward like a bridegroom. If you are a physician inditing a prescription, or a lawyer drawing a will, or a civil engineer putting down logarithmic matter, write in French prose: your patient will die, his testament be sustained, or an Eiffel Tower be erected to his memory in the correctest and clearest manner possible. But when you write a prayer, or exhort a forlorn hope, or put into

words any of those emotions that give life
its dignity, let your speech be English, that
your reader shall feel emotional elevation, his
heart lifted up within him, while his intellect
peers at what is beyond his reach.

If a man admits that for him poetry is the
chief part of literature, he must concede that
French prose cannot awaken in him those
feelings which he has on reading the English
Bible, Milton, Ruskin, Carlyle, or Emerson.
It is the alliance of our prose with our poetry
that makes it so noble. What English-speaking person in his heart thinks that any
French poet is worthy to loose one shoe-
latchet in the poets' corner of English shoes?

> " The man that loves another
>   As much as his mother tongue,
>   Can either have had no mother,
>   Or that mother no mother's tongue."

We have shown too much deference to this
inmate of clubs and weekly newspapers, this
international Frankenstein of literary cosmopolitanism. English poetry is the greatest
achievement in the world ; we think so, why
then do we make broad our phylacteries and
say that we do not? Ben Jonson says, "There
is a necessity that all men should love their

country; he that professeth the contrary
may be delighted with his words, but his
heart is not there." But we here concern
ourselves with another matter. We desire
to praise the two chief qualities that have
combined to make English literature so great:
they are common sense and audacity, and
their combined work is commonly called, for
lack of a better name, romance.

Younger brother to English poetry is English romance, which of all strange things in
this world is most to be wondered at. Brother
to poetry, cousin to greed, neighbor to idealism, friend to curiosity, English romance in
deed and word is the riches of the English
race. Its heroes march down the rolls of
history like a procession of kings : Raleigh
and Spenser, Drake and Sidney, Bunyan and
Harry Vane, Hastings and Burns, Nelson
and Sir Walter Scott, Gordon and Kipling.
Strange as English romance is, if a man
would learn its two constituent qualities in
little space, he need only take from the
library shelf " The Principal Navigations,
Voyages, Traffiques, and Discoveries of the
English Nation, made by Sea or Overland,"
compiled by Richard Hakluyt, Preacher.

Here we perceive the bond between romance, greed, idealism, and curiosity ; here we see how the British Empire plants its feet of clay upon the love of gain. Trade, trade, trade, with Russians, Tartars, Turks, with Hindoos, Hottentots, and Bushmen, with Eskimo, Indian, and South Sea Islander ; and yet hand in hand with greed go curiosity, love of adventure, and search for some ideal good. A wonderful people are the English so faithfully to serve both God and Mammon, and so sturdily to put their great qualities to building both an empire and a literature.

II

Who is not pricked by curiosity upon seeing " certeine bookes of Cosmographie with an universalle Mappe " ? Who is not splendidly content, of a winter evening, his oblivious boots upon the fender, his elbows propped on the arms of his chair, to read Mr. Preacher Hakluyt's Voyages? Who does not feel himself disposed " to wade on farther and farther in the sweet study of Cosmographie " ? Let us leave gallicized gallants, literary cosmopolites, their adherents and accomplices, and read old Hakluyt.

What quicker can attune the reader's attention to the valiant explorations that are to follow than to read that " when the Emperour's sister, the spouse of Spaine, with a Fleete of 130 sailes, stoutly and proudly passed the narrow Seas, Lord William Howard of Effingham, accompanied with ten ships onely of Her Majestie's Navie Roiall, environed their Fleete in most strange and warrelike sorte, enforced them to stoope gallant, and to vaile their bonets for the Queene of England " !

On the 9th of May, 1553, the ordinances of M. Sebastian Cabota, Esquier, Governour of the Mysterie and Companie of Marchants Adventurers, were all drawn up. The merchants aboard the ships were duly warned "in countenance not to shew much to desire the forren commodities; nevertheless to take them as for friendship; " and Sir Hugh Willoughby, Knight, Richard Chancellor, their officers, mariners, and company, set sail down the Thames in the Edward Bonaventure, the Bona Speranza, and the Confidencia, on their way by the northeast passage to Cathay. Before they had gone far, Thomas Nash, cook's mate on the Bona Speranza, was ducked at the yard's-arm for pickerie. The ships sailed up the North Sea, past Scandinavia, and into the Arctic Ocean, where Sir Hugh Willoughby and his two ships were lost, but Chancellor entered the White Sea, and landed in Russia. He then drove on sledges to Moscow, where he was received most graciously by his Majesty Ivan the Terrible. Chancellor wrote a description of the Russians, in which he tells their ways and customs. Although Chancellor could remember very well the days of Henry VIII. and the seizure of church lands, yet he remarks that when a rich Russian grows old " he shall be called before the Duke, and it shall be sayd unto him, Friend, you have too much living, and are unserviceable to your Prince, lesse will serve you, and the rest will serve other men that are more able to serve, whereupon immediately his living shall be taken away from him saving a little to find himselfe and his wife on; and he may not once repine thereat, but for answere he will say, that he hath nothing, but it is God's and the Duke's graces, and cannot say, as we the common people in England say, if wee have anything, that it is God's and our

owne. Men may say that these men are in
wonderful great awe and obedience, that
thus one must give and grant his goods
which he hath bene scraping and scratching
for all his life, to be at his Prince's pleasure
and commandement."

Coming back from his second voyage,
Chancellor brought an ambassador from Ivan
Vasilivich, Emperour of all Russia, Great
Duke of Smolenski, Tuerskie, Yowgoriskie,
Permskie, Viatskie, Bolgarskie and Sibierskie,
Emperour of Chernigoskie, Rezanskie, Polod-
skie, Rezewskie, Bielskie, Rostoskie, Yerasla-
veskie, Bealozarskie, Oudarskie, Obdorskie,
Condenskie, and manie other countries, to
the most famous and excellent Princes Philip
and Mary. (This patent inferiority of de-
signation was the cause of much diplomatic
correspondence.) Chancellor sailed out of
the White Sea through the Arctic Ocean;
for the Russians had no access to the Baltic,
as they had granted exclusive privileges to
the Flemings. Storms overtook him on the
Scottish coast : Chancellor and most of the
men were drowned ; only " the noble person-
age of the Ambassadour " was saved.

In 1557 Master Anthonie Jenkinson in

the Primerose, the Admirall, with three other
tall ships, took this ambassador back to Russia by the same northern way, seven hundred
and fifty leagues.   Jenkinson sailed up the
river Dwina in a little boat, lodging in the
wilderness by the riverside at night; and " he
that will travell those wayes, must carie with
him an hatchet, a tinderboxe, and a kettle,
to make fire and seethe meate, when he hath
it ; for there is small succour in those parts,
unless it be in townes."   He was graciously
received in Moscow by the Emperor about
Christmas time, and witnessed the court ceremonies.   At their Twelphtide, the Emperor
with his crown of Tartarian fashion upon
his head, and the Metropolitan attended by
divers bishops and nobles and a great con-
course of people, went in long procession to
the river, which was completely frozen over.
A hole was cut in the ice, and the Metropolitan hallowed the water with great solemnity,
and did cast of the water upon the Emper-
or's son and upon the nobility.   " That done,
the people with great thronging filled pots of
the said water to carie home to their houses,
and divers children were throwen in, and
sicke people, and plucked out quickly again,

and divers Tartars christened.   Also there were brought the Emperour's best horses to drink of the sayd hallowed water, and likewise many other men brought their horses thither to drinke, and by that means they make their horses as holy as themselves."

The English merchants were now well established in Muscovy, and sent home frequent reports about the manners and customs of Russians.   They noticed the Russian custom " every yere against Easter to die or colour red with Brazell a great number of egs ; the common people use to carie in their hands one of their red egs, not onely upon Easter day, but also three or foure days after, and gentlemen and gentlewomen have egs gilded which they cary in like maner.   When two friends meete, the one of them sayth, the Lord is risen, the other answereth, it is so of a truth, and then they kisse and exchange their egs both men and women, continuing in kissing 4 dayes together."

One of the agents of the company in Moscow, Master Henrie Lane, had a controversy with one Sheray Costromitskey concerning the amount of a debt due from the English merchants.   Lane proffered six hundred

rubles, but the Russians demanded double the
sum, and not agreeing they had recourse to
law. For trial by combat Master Lane was
provided with a strong, willing Englishman,
one of the company's servants; but the Russian champion was not willing to meet him,
and the case was brought to trial before two
chief judges. The English party were taken
within the bar, and their adversaries placed
outside. "Both parties were first perswaded
with great curtesie, to wit, I to enlarge mine
offer, and the Russes to mitigate their chal-
lenge. Notwithstanding that I protested my
conscience to be cleere, and their gaine by
accompt to bee sufficient, yet of gentlenes
at the magistrate's request I make proffer
of 100 robles more; which was openly com-
mended, but of the plaintifes not accepted.
Then sentence passed with our names in two
equall balles of waxe made and holden up by
the Judges, their sleeves stripped up. Then
with standing up and wishing well to the
trueth attributed to him that should be first
drawen, by both consents from among the
multitude they called a tall gentleman, saying: Thou with such a coate or cap, come
up: where roome with speede was made. He

was commanded to hold his cappe (wherein they put the balles) by the crown, upright in sight, his arme not abasing. With like circumspection they called at adventure another tall gentleman, commanding him to strip up his right sleeve, and willed him with his bare arme to reach up, and in God's name severally to take out the two balles; which he did delivering to either Judge one. Then with great admiration the lotte in ball first taken out was mine: which was by open sentence so pronounced before all the people, and to be the right and true parte. I was willed forthwith to pay the plaintifes the sum by me appointed. Out of which, for their wrong or sinne, as it was termed, they payd tenne in the hundred to the Emperour. Many dayes after, as their maner is, the people took our nation to be true and upright dealers, and talked of this judgement to our great credite."

Thus, with daring, good sense, and good luck, English commerce laid the foundation stones of the English Empire. But the reader must read for himself how these merchants flew the English flag for the first time across the Caspian Sea, and made their

way to Persia in the teeth of danger. Or
if the reader would learn more of English
courage, let him read that volume in which
Raleigh describes how Sir Richard Grenville
fought the Revenge.

We wish only to call attention to the
union of boldness and prudence in these English traders at the budding time of Elizabethan literature.

III

Commerce is like colonizing : it demands
manly virtue, forethought, audacity, quick-
ness to advance, slowness to yield ; it requires
diplomacy, flattery, lies, and buffets. Misadventure may follow misadventure, yet the
money-bags of England continue to propel
new adventurers over the globe. Merchant
adventurers do not seek Utopias, — let a man
plan a Utopia, and the English cut his head
off ; they seek a gay and gallant market, where
black, red, or yellow men will barter taffeta
and furs for English homespun, English glass,
and English steel ; or, better yet, will give
England a kingdom for " a cherry or a fig."
The money-getting English are no misers.
Their gold-bags breed audacity. Nobles of
Devon, franklins of Kent, burghers of Lon-

don, make many companies of merchant adventurers, and delight to risk their possessions for the sake of great returns. Half the famous ships that beat the Spanish Armada — the Bull, the Bear, the Dreadnaught, the Arkraleigh — were built for the commercial enterprise of piracy on the Spanish Main. Elizabeth and her nobles drew their ten per centum per mensem from such investments.

Money searched for cheap routes to Cathay, and opened up trade with Russia, Tartary, and Persia. Hope of gain sent colonists westward to Virginia, lured by the description of land " which will not onely serve the ordinary turnes of you which are and shall bee planters and inhabitants, but such an overplus sufficiently to be yielded, as by way of trafficke and exchaunge will enrich yourselves the providers, and greatly profit our owne countrymen." The swelling moneybags of England set Clive and Hastings over India, took the Cape of Good Hope, and sought twentyfold increase in Australia.

English commerce is no headstrong fool. It looks first, and leaps afterward. Like a wary captain, it takes its reckoning by com-

pass and sextant, and then spreads all sail.
It acts with the self-confidence of common
sense. Commerce is as prudent as Cecil and
as bold as Drake; but prudence is the controlling spirit. Common sense, also, is the
characteristic of English literature which has
exalted it so far beyond its modern rivals.
Powerful as have been its fantastic, monstrous, and metaphysical elements, disturbing
as have been affectation and demagogy, these
influences have been but little eddies whirling
round in the strong, steady current of common sense that has carried English literature
on its flood. Common sense unconsciously
recognizes that men are human; that imagination must play round the facts of daily
life; that poetry and prose must be wrought
out of the dust of the earth, and not out of
some heavenly essence. Common sense acts
upon instant needs, and meets the dangers
of the hour; it is not diverted from its path
by fears or allurements of the distant future;
it climbs like a child, clinging to one balus-
ter and then another, till it plants its steps
securely. There is a world of difference between it and " une certaine habitude raison-
nable qui est le propre de la race française en

poésie," according to Sainte-Beuve. One is bred in the closet by meditation; the other comes from living.

The good sense of Chaucer, Shakespeare, Dryden, Defoe, Pope, Fielding, Walter Scott, Tennyson, George Eliot, and others walls in English literature, so that it can stand the push of unruly genius in a Marlowe or a Shelley. Against this dominating common sense allegory rises in vain; passion cannot overtopple it; too subtle thought is sloughed off by it; dreams serve but to ornament; desires are tamed; parlor rhymesters are tossed aside. Common sense, with its trust in common humanity, has made English literature. The same solid wisdom which makes English money ballasts English verse and prose. There is an impress as of pounds, shillings, and pence on most of their pages; not vulgar and rude, as these words suggest, but like images on antique coins, stamped by conservatism, by precious things accumulated, by tradition and authority.

There is a certain melancholy about prudence; it bears witness to innumerable punishments suffered by ignorance and rashness, which must have been heaped up to a monstrous mass in order to create prudence as an instinct. But the worst punishments were administered before prudence appeared, and we reap the harvest. It is dismal and pathetic to think that common men should receive advantage from the sufferings of Marlowe, Greene, Peele, Chatterton, Byron, Shelley, and Poe. But after this manner runs the world away. English literature has been nourished by such sufferings, and the English Empire has also received from individuals all that they had to give. There is pathos in the reports sent by Hakluyt's traders to the home company. The investors dangle round Hampton Court, or sit in their counting-rooms in the city, while the adventurers leave England for years, brave hardships, risk disease and death, and send their duties back with humble hopes that their good masters in London may be content with what they do.

" Coastwise — cross-seas — round the world and back again,
  Whither the flaw shall fail us, or the Trades drive down:
Plain - sail — storm - sail — lay your board and tack
    again —
And all to bring a cargo up to London town !"

IV

Nevertheless, the desire to make money is not of itself capable of great action. It can put its livery upon a number of needy fellows who care not what they do, — who will trap beavers in Alaska, dig diamonds in Brazil, carry Hampshire kerseys to Tartars; but its main function is to be the utensil for the true adventurer: if he will sail, it builds a ship; if he will plant, it gives him seed; if he will rob, it loads him with powder and shot; it is the pack-mule that shall carry him and his equipment over the Alps of enterprise. The real strength of money lies in the wild spirits that will use it. Curiosity seeking the secrets of the world, daring looking for giant obstacles, conquerors in search of possessions whereto their courage shall be their title-deeds, — these must have money-getters. They publish abroad their needs that are to be, and farmers, miners, weavers, spinners, millers, smiths, and all grubbers spare and save, sweating to serve romantic adventurers.

The spirit of romance has flung its boldness into English literature. It plunders what it can from Greek, Latin, Italian, French, and Spanish. It ramps over the world : it dashes to Venice, to Malta, to Constantinople, to the Garden of Eden, to the Valley of the Shadow of Death, to Lilliput, to desert islands, to Norman baron and Burgundian noble, to Virginia, to Florence, to India, to the South Sea, to Africa, and fetches home to England foreign wealth by land and sea. How boldly it sails east, west, south, and north, and by its shining wake shows that it is the same spirit of romance that has voyaged from Arthurian legend to Mr. Kipling!

French men of letters have not had enough of this audacious spirit. They troop to Paris, where they have been accustomed to sit on their classical benches since Paris became the centre of France. The romance of Villon is the romance of a Parisian thief ; the romance of Ronsard is the romance of the Parisian salon. Montaigne strolls about his seigniory while England is topsy-turvy with excitement of new knowledge and new feeling. Corneille has the nobleness of a *jeune fille*. You can measure them all by their ability to plant a colony. Wreck them on a desert island, Villon will pick blackberries,

Ronsard will skip stones, Montaigne whittle, Corneille look like a gentleman, and the empire of France will not increase by a hand's-breadth. Take a handful of Elizabethan poets, and Sidney chops, Shakespeare cooks, Jonson digs, Bacon snares, Marlowe catches a wild ass: in twenty-four hours they have a log fort, a score of savage slaves, a windmill, a pinnace, and the cross of St. George flying from the tallest tree.

It is the adventurous capacity in English men of letters that has outdone the French. They lay hold of words and sentences and beat them to their needs. They busy themselves with thoughts and sentiments as if they were boarding pirates, going the nearest way. They do not stop to put on uniforms; whereas in France the three famous literary periods of the Pléiade, the Classicists, and the Romanticists have been three struggles over form, — quarrels to expel or admit some few score words, questions of rubric and vestments. The English have never balked at means after this fashion. Fénelon says of the French language " qu'elle n'est ni variée, ni libre, ni hardie, ni propre à donner de l'essor."

It is not fanciful to find this common element of daring in both English trade and poetry. English adventurers have sailed eastward and westward, seeking new homes for the extravagant spirits that find the veil of familiarity hang too thick over their native fields and cottages. Turn to the French: their merchants ply to Canada and India in vain. What sails belly out before the poetry of Ronsard or Malherbe? Into what silent sea is French imagination the first to break? The Elizabethan poets are a crew of mariners, rough, rude, bold, truculent, boyish, and reverent. How yarely they unfurl the great sails of English literature and put to open sea! The poor French poets huddle together with plummet in their hands, lest they get beyond their soundings.

No man can hold cheap the brilliant valor of the French. From Roncesvalles to the siege of Paris French soldiers have shown headlong courage. Nothing else in military history is so wonderful as the French soldiers from the 10th of August to Waterloo. Their dash and enterprise are splendid, but they do not take their ease in desperate fortune as if it were their own inn, as Englishmen

do. They have not the shiftiness and cunning that can dodge difficulties. They cannot turn their bayonets into reaping-hooks,
their knapsacks into bushels, their cannon
to keels, their flags to canvas. They have
not the prehensile hands of the English that
lay hold, and do not let loose.

English courage owes its success to its
union with common sense. The French
could send forty Light Brigades to instant
death; French guards are wont to die as if
they went a-wooing; but the French have
not the versatile absorption in the business
at hand of the English. The same distinction shows in the two literatures. Nothing
could be more brilliant than Victor Hugo in
1830. His verse flashes like the white plume
of Navarre. His was the most famous
charge in literature. Hernani and Ruy Blas
have prodigious brilliancy and courage, but
they lack common sense. They conquer,
win deafening applause, bewilder men with
excitement; but, victory won, they have not
the aptitude for settling down. They are
like soldiers who know not how to go back
to plough and smithy. The great French
literature of the Romantic period did not dig

foundation, slap on mortar, or lay arches in
the cellar of its house, after the English
fashion. Next to Victor Hugo, not count-
ing Goethe, the greatest man of letters in
Europe, of this century, is Sir Walter Scott.
Mark the difference between him and Hugo.
Scott's poetry and novels have a vigorous
vitality from his common sense, and therefore they are ingrained in the trunk of English literature ; the fresh sap of their romance quickens every root and adds greenery
to every bough. Victor Hugo is passionate,
imaginative, majestic, powerful, eloquent,
demagogical, but he does not stand the hard
test of squaring with the experience of common men.

Consider M. Zola, the greatest of living
French novelists, and we find the same lack
in him. His strong, sturdy talents have
fought a brilliant and victorious fight ; but
the brilliancy of his victory serves merely as
a light to rally his enemies ; he has offended
against the abiding laws of the common
knowledge of common men, and his books
have already passed the zenith of their glory.
There is hardly a famous man who does not
point the same moral. Michelet records the

introduction of tobacco. "Dès le début de cette drogue, on put prévoir son effet. Elle a supprimé le baiser. Ceci en 1610. Date fatale qui ouvre les routes où l'homme et la femme iront divergents." Read Renan's chapters upon King David. Take Racine, of whom Voltaire says "que personne n'a jamais porté l'art de la parole à un plus haut point, ni donné plus de charme à la langue française." He is noble, and appeals to the deepest feelings in men, — love, religion, heroism. By virtue of his spiritual nature he deserves great reverence, but he does not touch the understanding of common men. Ronsard, du Bellay, Clément Marot, have the same fault; they are witty, epigrammatic, musical, but they have not the one essential element. The two most successful French men of letters are the two possessing most common sense, Molière and Balzac.

Common sense is difficult to define, and suffers from a vulgar notion that it is totally separate and distinct from high virtues. It is Sancho Panza, but Sancho learned to appreciate Don Quixote. Common sense knows that it must be squire to the hero until the hero shall recognize his own dependence upon the squire. The wise and witty Voltaire failed in this respect, for he did not understand the daily need of idealism. Common sense sees the immediate obstacle which is to be overcome; in order to sharpen a pencil, instead of Durandal or Excalibur, it uses a penknife. Common sense trims its sails to catch the breeze, be it a cat's-paw, but it does not avoid the hurricanes of passion. Common sense uses common words; it husbands; it practices petty economies, so that the means of the hero shall be ample to his great enterprise. Of itself it can do little, but it makes straight the path for great achievement.

Jowett was fond of repeating Coleridge's remark that "the only common sense worth having is based on metaphysics." This saying is in part true, and it would not be over-curious to trace the indirect influence of metaphysics on the English Empire and on English literature.

V

There is no profit, however, in attempting to lug reason into this matter of the preference of English literature over French.

There is no justification here except by
faith. There is none to hold the scales,
while we heap English books into one to
outweigh French books in the other. Men
who have thrown off the bias of nationality
have disqualified themselves for the task, for
they have cut off all those prime feelings
and blind, indistinct sentiments that must
be the judges of last resort, and have set up
in their stead reason propped on crutches of
grammar, syntax, style, and euphony. In
fundamental matters, the intellect must take
counsel of the heart. Every man's memory
has stored in some odd corner the earliest
sounds of his mother's voice saying the
Lord's Prayer; it remembers the simple words
that first distinguished the sun and the moon,
buttercup and dandelion, Kai the bull ter-
rier and Sally the cat. No cultivation, no
sojourning in foreign lands, no mastery of
many books, can erase these recollections.
Some men there are whose conception of human relations is so large and generous that
to them the differences between peoples are
slight, when matched with the resemblances.
Such men are noble and lovable, but they
are not qualified to pronounce upon the

merits of two languages. Native language is restricting and confining so far as concerns peoples in international affairs, but it ennobles and enlarges fellow countrymen. Out of our native language are made our home and our country. The sweet sounds of speech heard only at home create our fundamental affections. The separation of nation from nation is a cheap price to pay for the great benefit which we of one people have received from the bond of common speech.

That which is true of language is true of literature. The great books for us are the books which we read when we were young; they bewitched us with our own language, they brought to us our English thoughts. The power of the English Bible is not the reward of merit only, — merit has never enjoyed such measure of success; it exists because we read it and re-read it when we were little boys. This early language of our mother and of our books is part of the " trailing clouds of glory " that came with us from our home. Love of it is a simple animal instinct, and the man who can proclaim himself free from it does not comprehend the riches of language or the great passions of life. We would alter a line of Wordsworth to fit this case : —

" We must be *bond* who speak the tongue that Shakespeare spake."

We cannot throw off the strong shackles that Shakespeare, the Bible, and all our English inheritance have put upon us; we are barred and bolted in this English tongue; only he who does not feel the multitudinous touch of these spiritual hands of the great English dead can stand up and say that the English and French languages are equal.

Mr. Matthew Arnold used to instruct us — as a professor of Hellenism was bound to do — that we must divest ourselves of national prejudices. We all admired him, and meant to mend our ways. He borrowed the word " saugrenu " from the French to tell us more exactly what manner of behavior was ours ; but faster than his prose pushed us on to international impartiality his poetry charmed us back. Mr. Arnold's poetry is essentially English; it is the poetry of an English Englishman. He is a descendant in direct line from Sidney, Herbert, Gray, Cowper, Wordsworth. He appeals to our native emotion ; he has English morals, English sentiment, English beliefs and disbeliefs ; his character is doubly emphasized by his occasional imitation of Greek forms. He has about him the atmosphere of the Anglican Church, — love of form, fondness for those emotions which are afraid to acknowledge instinct as their father, and yet shudder at logic. Mr. Arnold is an English poet, and for that reason we love him, and disregard his entreaties for cosmopolitan standards.

We are intolerant ; we are among those persons from whom bigots successfully seek recruits ; we have little respect, and rightly enough, for the free play of our reason ; we follow the capricious humor of our affections. We like old trodden paths, on whose rude bottoms we can still discern the prints of our fathers' feet. We are yeomen of the mind, as ready to throw our intellectual caps in the air for a Henry VIII. as for Hampden and liberty. We have the dye of conservatism ; we cannot hide it for more than a few sentences, and then only upon forewarning. We have just cause to fear that our behavior is bad in the presence of the sonnets of M.

José Maria de Heredia; we make faces when we read Verlaine. We cannot take those gentlemen as poets. They look to us like masqueraders, harlequins, unfairly brought from the darkness of the stage into the light of the sun. Try as we may to read an essay by M. Brunetière, a poem by M. Sully Prudhomme, or some French novel of the year, all is in vain. We must accept that condition of the mind to which it has pleased God to call us.

What a pleasure, after reading those books, to go back to old Hakluyt, and read aloud the lists of merchandise sent abroad or fetched home : item, good velvets, crimosins, purples and blacks, with some light watchet colours; item, ten or twelve pieces of westerne karsies, thicked well and close shut in the weaving and died into scarlet ; item, one hundred brushes for garments (none made of swine's hair) ; item, forty pieces of fine holland. What breaking of fences, what smashing of locks, what air, what comradeship, what a sense of poetry ! Surely, there is more poetry in the making of the English Empire than was ever printed in France.

Let us open wide the doors of our minds

and give hospitable reception to foreign literature whence soever it may come, but let us not forget that it only comes as a friend to our intelligence, and can never be own brother to our affections.

"A health to the native-born!"

DON QUIXOTE

DON QUIXOTE

IT is always good news to hear that new champions are coming forward to translate "Don Quixote" into English. It is a bold deed, well worthy a knight-errant of the pen; and if many men make the attempt, we may be perhaps so fortunate as hereafter to have a true English translation. "Don Quixote," it is said in the Encyclopædia Britannica, has been translated into every language in Europe, even including Turkish, but I cannot believe that any language is so fit as English to give the real counterfeit presentment of the book. One might guess that a Romance language would do better, but, on reflection, French prose lacks humor, and Italian has not sufficient subtlety to give the lights and shadows of "Don Quixote;" and as for German prose, in spite of Goethe it still is German prose. There is a scintilla of truth, so far as this translation is concerned, in the saying of Charles V., that French is the lan-

guage for dancing-masters, Italian for singing birds, and German for horses.   I should
like to be able to read the Turkish translation.   I imagine that there must be a dignity
and self-respect in the language that would
befit Don Quixote to a nicety; but for Sancho
it would not do, — he would be homesick
talking Turkish.

There are a number of English translations, — one by Mr. Shelton long ago, one
by Smollett, and others by Motteux, Jarvis,
Duffield, Ormsby, and Watts, — all more or
less inadequate, if I may judge from parts,
for I have never been so willful-blame as to
read them all.   In truth, the translation is a
very difficult matter.   Don Quixote himself
is one of the most delicately drawn characters in fiction ; almost every Spanish word he
speaks stands out in the reader's mind, separate and distinct, like a stroke in a Rem-
brandt etching.   How can you measure out
their English equivalents in the finely adjusted scales of language unless you have
ten talents for weights ?   Epigrams are commonly of little use in finding the way to
truth, but Coleridge has left a saying that,
I think, helps us materially in this matter of

translation. "Prose," he said, "is words in the best order; Poetry is the best words in the best order." Now, by what sleight of hand shall a man keep this best order of words in shifting thoughts from one language to another? In poetry we are waking up to this, and Homer and Dante are rendered into English prose. Now and again a man, if he have the luck to be a man of genius, may make English poetry when he professes to translate a foreign poet. Such a one was Mr. Fitzgerald. But I know of no one who has made both poetry and a translation, with a few exceptions: such as Shelley in his translation of the angels' chorus in "Faust," Dr. Hedge with Luther's hymn, and Wordsworth with Michelangelo's sonnet, "Ben può talor col mio ardente desio." Maybe the translators of the Old Testament were such.

Of all prose that I know, I should say that "Don Quixote" was the hardest to translate out of the original tongue; for Cervantes has used his words in the best order very often, and his Spanish tongue was of so fine a temper — for it had been framed among high-strung gentlemen, quick in quarrel, urbane

in manner, and of a broad human courtesy
such as gentlemen have in Utopia, and all
men, I needs must think, in heaven — that
the translator need be of a stout heart.
Words are delicate works. Nature has nurtured them, art has toiled over them. For
a thousand years those Spanish words have
been shaped by Spanish mouths, and now
some zealous translator, like a lean apothe-
cary, expects to catch their fragrance and
cork it up in English smelling-bottles. All
a nation's sentiment has gone into its words.
Great musicians, architects, painters, and
sculptors put into their works the feelings
of their country and of their age, but these
works remain the works of individuals and
bear their personal stamp, whereas all the
nation, at all times, from generation to generation, has been putting its passions into its
speech. The Spanish heart is not the English heart.

Moreover, the translator of Cervantes has
another great difficulty. Don Quixote is the
delineation of a man's character; he is as
real as any hero in fiction from Achilles to
Alan Breck, and much more so than the heroes who lie buried in Westminster Abbey.

" Er lebt und ist noch stärker
Als alle Todten sind."

This very reality lies in the arrangement
of words, and slips through the translator's
fingers. The hero was alive and then is
done into English, a process that has much
similarity to embalming. To draw the likeness of a living being in words is one of the
most difficult tasks in art. We all, no doubt,
can remember some figure coming, in the
days of our childhood, into our Eden from
the vague outer world, that impressed itself
deeply in our memories. Such a one I can
remember, — a delicately bred gentleman, one
of those in whom the gentle element was so
predominant that perhaps the man was pushed
too much aside. His bearing spoke of training and discipline received in some place
out of Eden that we knew not of, and there
was a manner of habitual forbearance, almost
shrinking, in his daily actions, as if he feared
that whatever he touched might turn to sorrow, which still kept us behind the line across
which his tenderness was ever inviting us.
I think to describe his smile and to translate " Don Quixote " would be tasks of like
quality.

But of all books in the world "Don Quixote" is the book for an English-speaking boy. There is a time in his boyhood while the sun of life throws a long shadow behind him, when, after he has read the Waverley Novels, Cooper, and Captain Marryat, he pauses, hesitating between Thackeray and Dickens. Which shall he take? The course is long, for a boy is a most just and generous reader. He reads his novelist straight through from start to finish, "David Copperfield," "Oliver Twist," "Nicholas Nickleby," "Old Curiosity Shop," and all, ending finally with a second reading of "Pickwick." That is the way novels should be read. Reading the first novel of one of the great men of literature is like Aladdin going down into the magic cave : it summons a genie, who straightway spreads a wonderful prospect before you, but it is not till the second or third book that you understand all the power of the master slave. It is at that moment of hesitation that "Don Quixote" should be put into the boy's hands; but that cannot be done now because there is no satisfactory English translation.

Of course, "Don Quixote" is a man's book,

also ; Cervantes has breathed into its nostrils
the breath of life, and, like the macrocosm,
it has a different look for the boy and for
the man of fifty. You can find in it the
allegory that the ideal is out of place in this
workaday world, that the light shineth in a
darkness which comprehendeth it not. You
can find the preaching of vanity, if such be
your turn of mind, in "Don Quixote" as well
as in the world. But the schoolboy does not
look for that ; there is no vain thing in life
for him, and perhaps his is the clearer vision.
And with this schoolboy, pausing as I have
suggested on the brink of Thackeray or
Dickens, a translation of "Don Quixote" has
the best chance of success. Its defects will
be of such a nature as will mar the man's
enjoyment, but not his. It will give him the
gallant gentleman pricked by a noble contempt for the ignoble triumphant and for
the acquiescent many ; he shall have there
the lofty disregard of facts that hedge in
housekeepers, barbers, and parsons ; he shall
find courage, endurance, knightliness, and
reverence for woman. After a boy has once
been squire to Sir Kenneth, to Ivanhoe, and
to Claverhouse, what business has he in life

but to right wrongs, to succor maidens, and
to relieve widows and all who are desolate
and oppressed? What if this gallant gentleman be a monomaniac, and be subjected
to disasters at the hands of farmyard louts
and tavern skinkers, by windmills and galley
slaves: must not Ivanhoe's squire march
through Vanity Fair and lodge in Bleak
House, his long breeches unentangled in
spurs, and his chief weapon of offense carried in his waistcoat pocket? Heine says
that he read "Don Quixote" for the first
time when a boy, and that then he "did not
know the irony that God put into the world,
and which the great poet had imitated in his
little world of print and paper." Heine is
mistaken; there is no question of knowledge
and ignorance. The boy has his world as
heavy to an ounce, weighed in scales of avoir-
dupois, as that of a man of fifty, and there
is no irony in it. The boy is not the subject
of illusion; there is in fact no irony there.
The man of fifty, *le soi-disant désillusionné*,
is certainly on the border of presumption, to
say that it is there, and then to call the boy
an ignoramus. To be sure, he commonly
couples his offensive epithet with some miti-

gating adjective, as " happy fool," or thus, "his pretty ignorance." But in place of the adjective there should be an apology. Every man is born into a house where there is a chamber full of veritable chronicles of Tristram and Launcelot, of Roland and Rinaldo di Mont' Albano ; and if his housekeeper, his barber, and his parson wall up the door and tell him that Freston the great enchanter has swooped down on dragon back and carried it off by night, his acceptance of their assertions and his lofty compassion for his old illusions furnish but poor proof of wisdom.

It is for the boy that a good translation should be made, and that might be done ; one in which Don Quixote shall talk like a scholarly gentleman, and in which there shall be no conscious grin of the translator spoiling the whole, as in that wretched version by Motteux. The boy wants two qualities in his books, enthusiasm and loyalty ; and here he has them jogging on side by side through four good volumes. Sainte-Beuve says that Joubert's notion of enthusiasm was *une paix élevée ;* a boy's idea is *la guerre élevée*, and Cervantes was of that mind. He was a soldier of the best kind, fighting for Europe

against Asia at Lepanto, and esteeming his
lost arm the most honorable member of his
body. Don Quixote is the incarnation of
enthusiasm ; and what loyalty was ever like
Sancho's, even to the deathbed where he
beseeches Don Quixote to live many years,
"for it would be the utmost foolishness
to die when no one had murdered him"!
There are many who are loyal to a friend's
deeds, and some to his faults, but to be
loyal to another's dreams and visions is the
privilege of very few. Besides, the boy demands incident, and here there is the greatest variety of adventure, of that delightful
kind that happens in La Mancha without
having to be sought in Trebisond or Cathay.

Another reason for a good translation is
that "Don Quixote" is the first modern novel.
It is the last of the romances of chivalry and
the first novel ; and as, on the whole, most
of the great novels are English novels (for
what other language can show a like richness to "Robinson Crusoe," "Tom Jones,"
"Rob Roy," "Pride and Prejudice," "Vanity
Fair," "David Copperfield," "Adam Bede,"
and "The Scarlet Letter"), there should be
an adequate English version of it. So many

novels of much skill and force are written nowadays that we are too often swayed in our judgment of them by the pulse of the year or of the decade. Were it not well, after reading Mr. Meredith or Mr. Moore, to take our bearings by a mark that has withstood the changing sentiments of ten generations of mortal men? " You cannot fool all the people all the time." Men during three hundred years are of so many minds, and have such diverse dispositions and temperaments, and are placed in such different circumstances, with various passions and prejudices, that any book that receives the suffrage of all is proved to be, to use Sainte-Beuve's phrase, *un livre de l'humanité.* By going back to these great human books we learn to keep our scales truly adjusted. Goethe said that every year he was wont to read over a play by Molière.

There have been a great many theories about the book, speculations as to what purpose Cervantes had in view when he wrote it. The chief two are that he intended a burlesque upon romances of knight-errantry, and that he intended an allegorical satire upon human enthusiasm. Doubtless he be-

gan with the purpose of ridiculing the old
romances, but, as Heine says, genius gallops
ahead of its charioteer. By the seventh
chapter he found himself with Don Quixote
and Sancho Panza seeking adventures in La
Mancha; he had in his heart a deep and
serious knowledge of life, and in his brain
wit and fancy such that the world has but
once had better, and he wrote. Men must
express the deep feelings within them : the
common man to one or two by words and
acts and silence, the man of genius to the
world by such means as nature has made
easiest for him. In Spain, since the invention of printing, the one form of popular
literature had been the romance of knight-
errantry. The three great cycles of romantic fiction — of King Arthur and the Round
Table, of Charlemagne and his Paladins, and
of the Greek empires founded by Alexander
the Great — had spread all over western
Europe, and had long before served their
office. Their place in Spain was filled by the
romances of knight-errantry. Of these, the
first and best was "Amadis of Gaul," which
was probably written in Castile about the
year 1350. The old version has been long

lost, but Garci-Ordoñez de Montalvo wrote
a new one some time after the conquest of
Granada, which obtained wide popularity
and still exists. The success of this was so
brilliant that a great many books were written in imitation of it. In the middle of the
sixteenth century these romances met with
two powerful enemies: one was the spirit of
the Catholic Reaction, the other the spirit of
classical culture. In 1543 Charles V. forbade
that any of these books should be printed
or sold in the West Indies, and in 1555 the
Cortes made its petition to the Emperor to
make the like law for Spain. The text of the
petition reads thus: " Moreover, we say that
it is most notorious, the hurt that has been
done and is doing in these kingdoms to young
men and maids and to all sorts of people
from reading books of lies and vanities, like
Amadis and all the books which have been
modeled upon its speech and style, also
rhymes and plays about love and other vain
things; for young men and maids, being
moved by idleness to occupy themselves with
these books, abandon themselves to folly,
and, in a measure, imitate the adventures
which they read in those books to have hap-

pened, both of love and war and other vanities; and they are so affected thereby that
whenever any similar case arises they yield
to it with less restraint than if they had not
read the books; and often a mother leaves
her daughter locked up in the house, thinking that she has left her to her meditations
(*recogida*), and the girl falls to reading
books of that kind, so that it were better
if the mother had taken her with her. . . .
And that it is to the great hurt of the con-
sciences, because the more people take to
these vanities, the more they backslide from
and cease to find enjoyment in the Holy,
True, and Christian Doctrine." Wherefore
the petition asks that no more such books
be printed, and that all those existing be
gathered up and burned, and that no book
be printed thereafter without a license; "for
that in so doing your Majesty will render a
great service to God, taking persons from
the reading of books of vanities, and bringing them back to read religious books which
edify the mind and reform the body, and
will do these kingdoms great good and
mercy." Mr. Ticknor and other commenta-
tors have gathered together condemnations

upon these romances uttered by various persons of note prior to the publication of "Don Quixote." There can be little doubt that these faultfinders were Puritans of the Catholic Reaction, and that the same spirit influenced the Cortes. In this same feeling the Puritans in England of Queen Elizabeth's time attacked the stage.

In the preface to Part I., Cervantes represents himself as sitting with his chin on his hand, pondering what he shall do for a preface, when a friend comes in, who, after making some rather dull suggestions, says, " This book of yours is an invective against books of knight-errantry ; . . . your writing has no other object than to undo the authority which such books have among the uneducated ; " and he ends with the advice, " Make it your purpose to pull to pieces the ill-based contrivance of these knight-errant books, which are hated by some, but praised by many more ; for if you accomplish this, you will have done a great deal." And Part II. ends with a declaration by Cide Hamete Ben Engeli (the author in disguise) that his "only desire has been to make men dislike the false and foolish stories of knight-errantry,

which, thanks to my true Don Quixote, are
beginning to stumble, and will fall to the
ground without any doubt." These are the
arguments for limiting and cutting down
the great purposes of the book, a commen-
tary on the life of man, to a mere satire upon
silly and extravagant romances; but the book
speaks for itself.

With respect to the other theory, that Cervantes intended a satire upon human enthusiasm, Mr. Lowell, in commenting, discovers
two morals: the first, "that whoever quarrels with the Nature of Things, wittingly or
unwittingly, is certain to get the worst of
it;" the second, "that only he who has the
imagination to conceive and the courage to
attempt a trial of strength with what foists
itself on our senses as the Order of Nature
for the time being can achieve great results
or kindle the coöperative and efficient enthusiasm of his fellow men." By this interpretation the condemnation of the quarrel is
itself condemned by the deeper moral. But
it little profits to seek after Cervantes' motives; he wrote about life, and he does not
draw any final conclusions. He observes
and writes. He tells of a gentleman who

found the world out of joint, and with a
"frolic welcome" proclaimed that he was
"born to set it right." The attempt is followed by the most disastrous and delightful consequences. Don Quixote is sometimes
triumphant, but many more times mocked,
mauled, persecuted, and despitefully used by
clown and duke, and Sancho shares all his
fortunes. Side by side go Imagination on
his hippogriff, and Common Sense on his
donkey. At the end of the book, the reader,
loving and admiring Don Quixote, loving
Sancho, and having rejoiced at every piece of
good fortune that has come to them on their
ill-starred career, hates and despises all those
who have ill used them, including those two
wiseacres the Parson and the Barber. If the
unoffending reader must draw a moral, he
would seem to hit near the mark by infer-
ring that enthusiasm justifies its own appel-
lation, and that the divine in us is the only
thing worth heeding and loving, though it
behave with lunacies inconstant as the moon,
or go to live with publicans and sinners.
But why draw a moral at all? Life is very
big, and there is less dogma now than there
used to be about the meaning or the worth

of it, and an observer of life may travel
about and note what he sees without being
compelled to stand and deliver his conclusions. What should we say if Cide Hamete
Ben Engeli had made an end in good Arabic
with " Life is but an integration of Matter
with a concomitant dissipation of Motion "?
Let the great books of the world escape these
hewers of epigrams and drawers of morals.
Hamlet has escaped to a place of safety; so
has the Book of Job. Faust is on the way
thither, and Don Quixote will one day keep
them company. It is a tale of life drawn
from the author's imagination, and it is
enough to know that a man who had lost an
arm in a sea-fight and had been a captive
slave for five years, who had been poor and
persecuted, began this joyous and merry history in prison, and continued it in the same
strain of joy and merriment to the end. Let
any man tired

> " to behold Desert a beggar born,
> And needy Nothing trimmed in jollity,"

betake himself to " *un lugar de La Mancha*." The very words conjure up spring-
time, holidays, and morning sun, and he
shall feel like the poet

"Quant erba vertz e fuehla par,
E l' flor brotonon per verjan,
E l' rossinhols autet e clar
Leva sa votz e mov son chan."

The joy of it is masculine and boyish; it maketh for life, like all good things. The reader never stops to think whether there be wit or humor, irony or optimism. These questionings are foisted upon you by the notes. If you read a Spanish edition, beware of the notes. Some there are who, in their schooldays, acquired a wise preference of ignorance to notes, but I have known many who would stop in the middle of a sentence to read a note, and then begin again exactly at the asterisk where they had left off. The notes in the editions by the Spanish Academy, Dr. Bowle, Pellicer, and Clemencin are all to be skipped.

In Don Quixote we believe that we have a partial portrait of Cervantes. He has described somewhere his own physical appearance in a manner very like to the description of the knight, and in the latter's character we feel sure that we have the real Cervantes. Certainly there is there the likeness of a high-spirited Spanish gentleman at a time when Spanish gentlemen were the first in the world. Every little detail about the knight is told with such an intimate affection that Cervantes must have been writing down whatever he believed was true of his own best self. The ready knowledge with which he wrote is manifest from the carelessness with which he makes mistakes, as with Sancho's ass, on which Sancho suddenly mounts half a page after losing him forever, and in the names of la Señora Panza, and in various details. Certainly Cervantes is very fond of Don Quixote, and does him justice ; and he has a kindliness for the reader, too, and pays him for his sore sympathies every now and then by the joyous feeling of victory which he receives when Don Quixote, in the midst of a company that think him mad, delivers a brilliant harangue, leaving them confounded and the reader exultant. Sancho said Don Quixote ought to have been a parson, and you feel that he would have adorned any position of dignity within the gift of the Majesty of Spain. The art with which the story is told and the characters are drawn grows upon one's wonder. For example, Don Quixote has been lowered down into the cave of Montesinos, and after some hours, during which Sancho has become much alarmed for his master's safety, he reappears and gives an account of the most marvelous adventures. Sancho and the reader are aghast; they know that the adventures cannot be true, and they know equally well that Don Quixote is incapable of telling a lie, and the wonder is whether he is mad or has been dreaming. This same wonder finally overtakes Don Quixote, and you feel, without being told, that he is struggling with his memory to find out what did really happen as he faces the awful possibility that what he related may not have been true. There is a certain low fellow in the book, one Samson Carrasco, a friend of the Parson and the Barber, of good purposes, but of no imagination, who devises a scheme to fetch Don Quixote home. This plan was to arm himself as a knight-errant and take Don Quixote captive. The approach of the combat is very disagreeable; you cover over with your hand the lines ahead of where you are reading, so that you may not read faster than you shall acquire fortitude to bear whatever may happen. And behold, Rosinante breaks into a gallop, dear horse, — Boiardo and Bucephalus never did as much, — and the counterfeit knight is hurled to the ground. By the same dull device this vulgar Carrasco finally, near the end of the story, ran atilt with Don Quixote and unhorsed him. He dismounted, and stood over our hero with his spear. The terms of the combat were that he who was conquered should confess that the other's lady was the more beautiful. "Don Quixote, without raising his visor, with weak and feeble voice, as if he were speaking from within a tomb, replied: 'Dulcinea of Toboso is the most beautiful woman in the world, and I am the most miserable knight on earth, and it were not right that the truth should suffer hurt from my weakness; thrust home your lance, Sir Knight, and since you have taken my honor, take away my life also.'" It were difficult to imagine that this is a satire upon human nature, and that Cervantes made mock of the spirit of chivalry.

One of the deepest and most delightful elements of the book is the relation between Don Quixote and Sancho Panza; in fact, it is Sancho's obedience, his profound loyalty

and belief in his master, that throw both
their characters into high relief : and here
lies one of the hardest tasks for the translator ; for unless their conversations are given
with the delicacy and grace of the original,
they cease to be Don Quixote and Sancho,
and become mere comic figures.

Sancho has never had full justice done to
him. Affection and regard he has had in fair
measure, no doubt. One loves him as one
loves a dog ; not the noble, fair-limbed, fine-
haired aristocrat, but the shag-haired little vil-
lain, *nullius filius*, who barks at your guests,
and will gnaw a drumstick in my lady's chamber unless he be prevented. But Sancho's
character and intelligence have not had their
due. He is commonly spoken of as if he
were one of old Gobbo's family, selfish and
of loutish appetites ; but in truth he is not
related at all. Sancho stands charged with
greediness ; and as to eating, he ate well
whenever he had an opportunity, but he
worked very hard and needed food, for he
often went supperless to bed, and was never
sure of the morrow. His desire to be *gober-
nador* was the imperial fault of ambition,
and most honorable ; and when he governed

Barataria, he bore his great office meekly, and was a just and beneficent ruler. When Don Quixote first told him of the great fortunes, even of a royal complexion, that sometimes fall to the lot of the esquire to a knight-errant, his first thought was that Teresa Panza would be queen and his children princes. His intelligence bloomed and unfolded under the sunny influence of Don Quixote's company; in fact, one of the most delightful things in the whole book is the elevation of Sancho's understanding as he travels from Part I. into Part II. Preface-makers say that Cervantes discovered how popular Sancho was, and, taking his cue accordingly, developed and expanded Sancho's wit and gifts of speech; but the true reason is that living with a dreamer of dreams ennobles the understanding. When Don Quixote had forbidden the brutal laborer to thrash the boy, and made him promise by the laws of knighthood, the boy said, "My master is no knight; he is rich John Haldudo, and he lives in Quintanar." "No matter," replied Don Quixote; "the Haldudos may become knights; every man is the child of his own actions." By his faithfulness and loyalty to his master, Sancho's condition was made gentle and his intelligence was quickened. Even in the beginning Sancho is by no means backward in comprehension. Don Quixote resolves to get a sword that will cut through any steel and prevail over all enchantment. Sancho apprehends that the virtue of the sword may be personal to Don Quixote, and of no avail to him, as he is only an esquire. And he explains that the reason why Don Quixote was horribly beaten by the Yanguesian cattle-drivers was that he had neglected to observe his vow not to eat baked bread or do sundry other things until he should have obtained Mambrino's helmet. Don Quixote quietly replies that that is so, and that Sancho was beaten also for not reminding him. Sancho has a generous human sympathy, too; for when Don Quixote finds Cardenio's love-letter, he asks him to read it aloud " *que gusto mucho destas cosas de amores.*" The difference in their views of life, however, and the help they render each other in getting into difficulties, is the precious quality of the book.

There are a hundred men who admire and reverence Dante for his fierce seriousness and

burning convictions about life, to one who
would feel that the like reverence and admiration were due to the laughing seriousness
and smiling convictions of Cervantes. Heine
somewhere draws a picture of the gods din-
ing and Hephæstos limping among them to
pour out the wine, while their laughter floats
off over Olympus, when suddenly in the
midst of them stalks a Jew and flings down
a cross upon the banquet-table, and the
laughter dies. But with the revolving years
laughter has once more come to take its place
as a divine attribute, and Cervantes' seriousness, his sympathy and loving-kindness, may
set him, in the estimation of men, as high, as
wise, as deep, as Dante. I think with what
pleasure he and Shakespeare met in the
Happy Isles and laughed together, while
Dante, *a guisa di leone*, sat sternly apart.
What happier time was there ever in those
Islands of the Blest than that sweet April
wherein those two landed from Charon's
bark? For surely Shakespeare's spirit tar-
ried a few days that they might make their
voyage and entrance together. In Cervantes,
says Victor Hugo, was the deep poetic spirit
of the Renaissance. In him was the milk of

loving-kindness. After reading his book, we see a brighter light thrown on the simple human relations, the random meetings of men and women in this world of ours that is not so unlike to La Mancha, and we become more sensitive to the value of words spoken by human lips to human ears, and of the touch of the human hand in our greetings and partings. It is not the usage among soldiers to confess their own tenderness, and Cervantes has thrown over his confession the veil of irony. Heinrich Heine did the like. These proud men would not have their women's hearts show on their sleeves, and they mocked the world. It was easily done.

> " Diese Welt glaubt nicht an Flammen,
> Und sie nimmt's für Poesie."

In Algiers, Cervantes, with some of his fellow captives, devised several plans of escape, all of which failed, and he was threatened with torture if he would not disclose the names of the conspirators and the story of the plot. He told nothing but that he alone was responsible. So he did; so he wrote. He obeyed the great prayer made to each of the children of men: " Simon, son of Jonas, lovest thou me? Feed my sheep."

A HOLIDAY WITH MONTAIGNE

A HOLIDAY WITH MONTAIGNE

IT was my good luck to spend my last holidays with two companions. One was my canoe, — a canvas canoe painted maroon. Its paddle has but one blade. There is a seat for another paddler in the bow, and room amidships for a passenger to lie quite comfortable. It is somewhat difficult for one to paddle a canoe meant for two. You put your kit and a bag of sand in the bow, lean a little to one side, and take your strokes as even as you can. In this way, in calm weather, you make good speed; but when the wind blows a few points off the bow, nothing but great experience or sudden genius will help you. The canoe moves as if of a sudden it had heard music from Venusberg; it whirls about, once, twice, and breaks into a jig; then frolicking with the wind, pirouettes back whence you came, bobbing its bow like a dancing-master. "Certes c'est un subject merveilleusement vain, divers et ondoyant que" le canot.

I started at the southern end of Lake George. The cars had been hot, and the freight-master and expressman had both laid violent hands on my canoe. From them I rescued it only by paying fees under duress, which were subsequently returned to me by persons in authority. The sun was high, a light breeze blew upon my back, a soft gray cloud hung over me like an umbrella. My pack and the sand-bag balanced my stroke. My sandwiches and a bottle of soda-water lay safe in a tin pail under the seat. The blue-gray hills rose sleepily in the distance. The trees on the shore bunched themselves into indistinctness, and hid all but the chimneys of the houses. A noisy, self-assured little launch puffed up to us, and finding us in all points uninteresting, whistled off up the lake. I became perfectly content.

My other companion, carefully covered by a rubber blanket, lay still a little forward of the middle thwart. He was very fine in a new half-calf binding, which he had got from the money saved by the economy of a foot in the length of the canoe. The lake was so smooth that there was no danger of water-drops, and I took off the rubber blanket that

I might see him.   He looked very dignified
in his bronze-and-black covering.   I had
been told that a canoe trip offered me a rare
opportunity to learn what science in one of
its branches had been doing of late, — science in popular dress humbling itself to the
level of lewd persons, like Shakespeare's Bol-
ingbroke on a holiday.

But I preferred the companionship of letters, and only hesitated as to whether I should
take with me a man of the world or a credu-
lous believer.   In the city, a believer is most
sympathetic.   We like to hear a man dare to
affirm and be simple, to take his oath that
the sky is blue, the earth solid, that right is
right, and assert dogmas on heights, depths,
and breadths ; we cry out for a St. Paul, an
Emperor Julian, a Wendell Phillips ; we care
little as to the content of the beliefs, but we
cannot stomach the irresolute middle ground.

> " Questo misero modo
> Tengon l' anime triste di coloro,
> Che visser senza infamia e senza lodo."

We like to hear men trundle their push-carts
up and down Broadway and Tremont Street,
hawking old creeds.   Give us anything which
will protect us against the incessant rolling

and pitching of unstable thought. In the
city it is not well to cope with a man of the
world, we shrink before "son don de sou-
rire de son œuvre, d'y être supérieur." He
has us at a disadvantage and presumes upon
it; he turns all the happenings among crowding men and women into parables for his
triumph and our discomfiture.

In the country all this is reversed. In
quiet and fresh air, dogmas grow heavy as
poppy and mandragora; they vex us. Why
should we join this guild of thought, that
club of notions, that body metaphysical?
We turn impetuously to the man of the
world; his knowledge can no longer put us
out of countenance, his experience is no better than an oyster fork in a jungle. Inevit-
ably I rushed to Montaigne, and was justified. Nothing is more delightful than to be
with Montaigne on water and under trees;
he ceases to have any of the superciliousness
of a man of the world, and plays the elder
brother come back from far travel and from
meeting many men. No matter how often
you may have read him in town, he is more
kind, more genuine, more simple, when you
meet him in this way and hear him talk at

ease. It is a constant pleasure to find how quick is his sympathy with happiness, how keen his compassion for sorrow.

Lake George is pretty well surrounded by a cordon of houses, but by a discriminating course these may be avoided. There is a little cove hid behind a point of land, which, beaked with a rock, juts into the lake. It is hard by a house marked " The Antlers " on the map. This map you buy in the cars from the newsboy. It is the appendix to a book containing a eulogy on Lake George. Leave the eulogy on the seat ; the map is very useful. This little cove has a graveled edge whereon to beach the canoe. From the rocky beak you dive into three fathoms of transparent water down towards the blue-green rocks at the bottom. After that sandwiches and soda-water. Next a pipe filled with long cut, and opening volume one, the spirit of Michel de Montaigne sits beside you discoursing. A skeptic, using the word with reference to life in general, is intended to mean one whose ideas have no home, but travel from inn to inn like wandering Jews ; a man whose mind is like a fine lady before a milliner's mirror, who tries on one bonnet

after another, looks at it before and behind,
over the shoulder, at this angle and that,
but cannot prevail upon herself to say, I take
this, this is mine. And as this word "skeptic" is commonly used of one with whom the
speaker finds some fault, it carries a tinge of
ill; it signifies a person who does not believe that men act from disinterested motives,
does not recognize the importance of human
feelings, who denies the dignity of human
existence, — one in whose presence we are
ashamed of our love for the melodramatic.

The greatest believer in humanity that
has ever lived in Europe is Shakespeare. If
a man be morbid, if somebody's toes tread
upon the kibes on his heel, if he be disheart-
ened by ill success in his government of life,
and, like the blind man beating the post, can
discover no virtue in men and women, he be-
takes himself to Shakespeare. There he finds
the dignity of man written in capital letters.
So it is with the books of all great men, or
perhaps one should say of all great men
whose fame and books have lived. Men and
women do not cherish those who despise
them. The books of misanthropes lie un-
read in national museums. Dust to dust.

There is no resurrection for them.   Therefore one has a right, in approaching a man
whose books are on the shelves of every library, to assume that he is not a skeptic in
any unworthy sense.   To judge a man, mark
what interests him.   Positive testimony, as
lawyers say, outweighs negative evidence.
In his discourse De la Tristesse, Montaigne
tells how, after his capture by Cambyses,
Psammenitus watched with apparent serenity
his son marched to death, his daughter borne
away a slave, but on beholding one of his
servants maltreated burst into weeping.   It
might be thought, says Montaigne, that his
fortitude, equal to the first sorrows, had at
last been overcome, as the last straw breaks
the camel's back.   But when Cambyses questioned him, Psammenitus answered, " It is
because this last displeasure may be mani-
fested by weeping, whereas the two former
exceed by much all meanes and compasse to
be expressed by teares."   He tells so many
anecdotes of this kind that we are bound to
reject the word " skeptic " as applicable to
Montaigne in any mean and narrow sense.

If there be in him one quality more than
another that wins the affection of the reader,

it is a certain manner of courtesy, of hospitality, familiar, yet of trained urbanity, which infects all these discourses. The reader finds that Montaigne is wise, but he meets no suggestion that he himself is foolish; he discovers that Montaigne is of wide experience, and he does not stop to think it odd that this experience, though so broad, tallies at all points with his own, which, had he stopped to think, he would have known to be narrow. It is with such skill and good breeding that your host leads you from matter to matter. He spreads before you one thing after another with the freshness and unexpectedness of a conjurer who suddenly out of your own memory produces meditations and reflections which you had not known were there. It is as if you were both ruminating upon a theme of common experience. Intermingled with his stories and reflections, his talk about himself, with its apparent self-revelation, pleases us wholly. Montaigne affects to wish us to believe that the book is about himself. He keeps repeating, " C'est moy que je peins." " These are but my fantasies, by which I endeavour not to make things knowen, but myselfe." " Others fashion man, I repeat him;

and represent a particular one but ill made."
While the book is in your hand, this egotism,
or rather, say friendliness, seems to indicate
a discriminating intimacy with you, giving
you to feel that, unconsciously as it were, he
bends and unfolds himself in consequence of
the atmosphere of your personality. It is
this flattery in his urbanity that has made
people believe in his simplicity and sincer-
ity. Readers should be guileless as children,
simple, innocent, unsophisticated. And it
may be that Montaigne is genuine. Breeding need not displace nature. Montaigne
does not become a double-dealer because his
manners are good and put us at our ease.
One is a little ashamed to question Montaigne's portrait of himself. Yet it is hard
not to do so, for he has the manner of a
well-graced actor. There is no imputation
of ill upon Montaigne in suggesting that he
does not give us his real picture. Unless
a man's heart be pure gold, the public weal
does not demand that he wear it on his
sleeve. Moreover, it may be that Montaigne
endeavors to draw himself, and yet, his talents not permitting, does not. Howbeit, his
manner has a perpetual charm. One would

have young men fashion their outward behavior upon M. de Montaigne.

From this little cove near " The Antlers " there are some seven miles to the Narrows, and it is well worth while to cover them before sunset, in order to see the shadows from the western hills crawl up on those to the east. It means a steady and industrious paddle. I had consulted the map as to where to spend the night, and had determined upon the clump of houses denominated "Hulett's;" for the size of the asterisk on the map seemed to import an inn or a lodging-house, and suggested to my luxurious mind generous accommodations, — perhaps Bass's ale for dinner, and a bath. The wind blew from behind quite fresh. I tucked Montaigne well under his blanket, tilted the canoe slightly to the side I paddled on, and watched the gradual sinking of the sun and the little splashes of the waves as they ran beside me. After a paddle of a number of miles comes fatigue between the shoulder-blades; it can be likened to nothing but a yoke or the old man that sat astraddle of Sindbad's neck. On feeling this yoke, to obtain relief, you paddle on the other side of the boat. A better remedy

is to take a swim. The wind blew fast up
the Narrows, and I was thankful it came to
aid me, for I could not have made head
against it. Spray from the wave-tops spat-
tered into the canoe, and it was hard to keep
it steady. It was as if the bow had a potent
desire to look round at me. First it swerved
to right, then to left, and after trying this
succession for a number of times, lulling me
into routine and security, after a turn to starboard it made believe to turn as usual to
port; but just when my paddle was ready to
meet that manœuvre it swung back to starboard, spattering the water so thick that
Montaigne stood well in need of his blanket. Then the canoe lay limp, as if it were
completely exhausted and wholly meritorious,
like Roland in the market-place at Aix.
Every wave tipped it to and fro, while I
brandished the paddle to right and to left
to keep from shipping enough water to sink
me. After a few minutes, like a puppy that
has been playing dead dog, it jumped to
what would have been its keel if it had had
one, and shot on over the water. The setting sun shed a golden brown over the hill-
tops to the east; under the shadow-line the

trees passed into gloom, and haze rose from the water's edge as if to hide a troop of Undines coming forth from their bath. To the west, against the ebbing light, the hills stood out black, and the little islands passed quickly by dotted with wooden signs, "government property," which looked in the distance like gray tombstones. I went ashore to lie down, rest, and read for a few minutes before dark. It may be the trees, the wind moving among the leaves, the jagged outline of the leaves themselves, or merely the smell of the pines, it may be the water of the lake rippling over the changing colors of the stones, it may be the sky framed by the boughs overhead, or it may be all in combination, yet by them and in them a man grows wiser, his limitations relax their tentacles and loose their hold,

> "While with an eye made quiet by the power
> Of harmony and the deep power of joy
> We see into the life of things."

Nature proffers a test of genuineness for a book the like of which cannot be found elsewhere. Out of doors, amid the simpler life of earth, motives for deception fail, masks are cumbersome; disguises grow too heavy to wear, and are transparent at that. By some strange power, the inner reality throws its shine or shadow through the man's waistcoat, through the book's cover, over the outer semblance. The pine is the clearest-eyed tree of all trees. Its needles are so many magnets pointing towards the truth. Read Cervantes under the pine-tree, and you will find the marks of Don Quixote's heels and lance-butt fresh in the moss. Read Dante there after the sun has set, when the light begins to fail and the chill wind rises, and you must stop your ears against the "sospiri, pianti, ed alti guai." It makes one marvel to mark how sensitive the pine-tree is to its company. Its tones, its shape, its colors, vary; it draws in its needles and protrudes them as if it fetched deep breaths. Its voice has the bass notes of seriousness and the treble of a boy's merriment. The deep brown resin on its trunk holds the light as if there were fire within. I think there is a strain of Clan Alpine in us all; we owe allegiance to the pine.

Perhaps Montaigne does not sympathize with great emotions, but he is interested, deeply interested, in the drama of human

existence ; he has the instinct of dramatic
feeling ; he cares not only for the free play
of life, but also for a particular outcome ; he
prefers one issue to another : not that Virtue
should be rewarded and Vice punished, but
that Prudence should be happily married and
Folly be pointed at.   Common Sense is the
god of his divinity.

Pascal complains, " Montaigne parloit trop
de soi."   A grievous fault if a man lack
charm, but Montaigne is charming.   One
would not that young Apollo — he that is
killing a lizard on a tree-stump — should
wear jacket and trousers.   Montaigne makes
no pretense of self-effacement.   He says, I
will write about myself.   He embroiders
" Ego " on his banner, and under that sign
he has conquered.   If men dislike apparent
egotism, let them leave Montaigne.   Such
men should vex themselves at all expression,
for all fiction and art are ripe with personality.   But is this portrait of Montaigne by
himself really indicative of egotism ?   For
my part, it is as if Boswell had found Dr.
Johnson in himself.   Here is a man with a
rare gift of delineation.   He sits for his own
portrait.   But above this rare gift and con-

trolling it sits the indeterminate soul; and as essay succeeds essay, this soul, uncertain of itself, half mocking his readers, half-mocking himself, says, Here is the portrait of Michel de Montaigne; but if you ask me, reader, if it be like me, — eh bien, que sçay-je?

In half an hour I was in the canoe again, laboring vigorously. After a paddle in rough waters of half a dozen miles a man of ordinary brawn begins to think of shore. The sun had set, the western light had faded and gone. The stars were out. Hulett's, with its cold bath, cool ale, and hot beef-steak, began to stand out very clear and distinct before my mind's nose and eyes, but there were no physical signs of it. Hulett's has a post-office, and in view of this governmental footing it is, to my thinking, under a sort of national obligation to shine out and be cheerful to all wayfarers by land and water. I kept my eyes fixed over the starboard bow. The miles grew longer; ordinary miles became nautical. The yoke upon my neck would not budge, shift the paddle as I might. The wind dropped down; the water reflected Jupiter looking out through a rift in the clouds; the widening lake lay flat to the shore, over which hung a blackness that I took to be the outline of the hills. The monotony of the stroke, usually so favorable to reflection, played me false. The beat of the paddle, which during the day had had a steady half-musical splash, and had scattered drops like the tang of a rhyme at the end of every stroke, made no sounds but bath — bath — bath — Bass — Bass — Bass — Hu — Hu — Hu — letts — letts — letts. But no lights; only the flat water and the dark outline widening out. Montaigne vanished from my mind. I thought of nothing, and repeated to myself solemnly, " A miss is as good as a mile, — a miss is as good as a mile ; " wondering what conclusion I could draw from this premise. Lights at last. First one, which grew and expanded and divided in two, then in four, and other lights appeared beyond. In a few minutes I dragged the canoe up on a little beach, tipped it upside down, tucked a volume of Montaigne under my arm, slung my night-pack on my paddle, and approached a piazza and voices. I skirted these, and reached a back door. A low growl elicited a pleasant

"Be quiet," from some one in authority.
The light streamed from the opened door.
I explained my desires, and received a short
answer that this house took lodgers, but that
it was very particular, and " what's more,
the house is full." I guessed that my appearance made against me. I trusted that
my speech was better than my clothes, and
tried to remember what I could of travelers
in distress. I felt for my purse. A very
worn and dingy leather met my fingers. I
withdrew my hand and talked fast, recalling
how Ulysses' volubility had always stood him
in good stead. I was successful. The house
expanded, put forth an extra room; a tub
was found, also chops and Milwaukee beer.

What a blessing is the power of recuper-
ation in man! Dinner done, I lighted my
pipe and fell into discourse with Montaigne.
This after-dinner time is the time of all the
day to sit with Montaigne. The mind rests
at ease upon its well-nourished servant, and
lack of desire begets interest. You yield
to the summons of *bien-être ;* the land of
socialists, of law, of railroads and time-tables,
bows and withdraws, leaving you alone in
the world of leisure. More than in other

worlds Montaigne is at home here. His
voice has leisure in it. The titles of his discourses, " Of Sadnesse," " Of Idlenesse,"
" Of Lyers," " Whether the Captaine of a
Place Besieged Ought to Sallie Forth to Par-
lie," " Of the Incommodity of Greatnesse,"
are leisurely ; his habit is leisurely. Leisure
sits in his chair, walks when he walks, and
clips out anecdotes from Plutarch for him.
Bordeaux, during his mayoralty, must have
abounded in trim gardens. Yet there is nothing lazy here. Jacques Bonhomme may
be lazy, *bourgeois gentils-hommes* may be
lazy, but Montaigne has leisure. As you
read you have time to contemplate and reflect ; you are not impatient to pass through
the garnishment of his essay and come to
the pith, in which you believe that Montaigne will most truly say what he truly
thinks. Here is the intellectual charm of
the book, — out of all he says to lay hands
upon his meaning and ascertain his attitude.
The problem is ever present. Is there an
attempt on his part, by an assumed self-
revelation, to mislead, or does the difficulty
lie in his very genuineness and simplicity ?
Does his belief lie concealed in his anec-

dotes, or is it set forth in his egotistical sentences ? Is he playing his game with you,
or only with himself ? To my mind, it is
as if he divided himself and were playing
blind-man's buff ; one half blindfolded, grop-
ing and clutching, the other half uncaught
still, crying, "Here I am ! " The same impression is left whether he talks of himself
or suggests theories of life and death.
" The world runnes all on wheeles. All
things therein moove without intermission ;
yea, the earth, the rockes of Caucasus, and
the Pyramides of Ægypt, both with the
publike and their own motion. Constancy
it selfe is nothing but a languishing and
wavering dance. I cannot settle my object ;
it goeth so unquietly and staggering, with
a naturall drunkennesse. I take it in this
plight, as it is at th' instant I ammuse my
selfe about it. I describe not the essence but
the passage ; not a passage from age to age,
or as the people reckon, from seaven yeares
to seaven, but from day to day, from minute to minute. My history must be fitted
to the present." Is not this sense of uncertainty the very effect Montaigne wishes to
leave upon the reader's mind ? And how

could he do it better than by putting forth a portrait of himself, saying, This is according to the best of my knowledge, and refusing to say, This is a true picture? If a man, set to the task of describing himself, cannot accomplish it, what assurance of correspondence have we between things in themselves and our knowledge, which for the most is nothing but portraits of things drawn by others, and coming to us through a succession, each copy in which is stamped with uncertainty? Has he not left this portrait of himself as the great exemplar of his doctrine? It is his secret. Whatever it be, it is his humor, his chosen method of expression. I believe he wishes to tell the reader about himself, but cannot be sure that he is showing himself as he is. He found much pleasure in trying to explain himself by sayings and stories gathered from Plutarch. There was something in the ingenuity of the method that gratified him.

There could be no better evidence of the work and anxiety spent upon these essays than that given by a comparison of the two first editions. Montaigne wrote them and rewrote them. One can feel the hesitation

and deliberation with which he chose his
words. He says : " It is a naturall, simple,
and unaffected speech that I love, so written
as it is spoken, and such upon the paper as
it is in the mouth, a pithie, sinnowie, full,
strong, compendious, and materiall speech,
not so delicate and affected as vehement and
piercing. Rather difficult than tedious, void
of affectation, free, loose and bold ; not Pe-
danticall, nor Frier-like, nor lawyer-like, but
rather downe right, as Suetonius calleth that
of Julius Cæsar." The French men of letters in the seventeenth century thought that
Montaigne had no art, and in England,
George Savile, the distinguished Marquis of
Halifax, in accepting the dedication of Cot-
ton's translation, says : He " showeth by a
generous kind of negligence that he did not
write for praise, but to give the world a true
picture of himself and of mankind. . . . He
hath no affection to set himself out, and
dependeth wholly upon the natural force of
what is his own and the excellent application
of what he borroweth." With great respect
let it be said that this is a mistake. Montaigne had great art, and not art alone, but
arts and artifice of all kinds. Every great

book is a work of art. Every book that survives its own generation is a work of art.
No one knew this better than Montaigne.
He desired immortality, and wrote to that
end. His book is the fruit of hard labor, of
thought deliberate, considerate, affectionate;
it has been meditated awake, and dreamed
upon asleep; cogitated walking, talking,
afoot, and on horseback. Nothing in it has
been left to chance and the minute. The
manuscript at breakfast was his newspaper,
after dinner his cigar; out of doors it was
in his pocket, it lay under his pillow at
night.

Sitting in his library in the third story
of the château's tower, pacing up and down
the corridor leading to it, cantering on his
comfortable cob, promenading in his vege-
table garden, you would think him as far
and safe from disturbance as from the vol-
canoes in the moon. Yet when he betook
himself to his château it was but twelve
months before the massacre of St. Bartholomew. Leaguers and Huguenots, men with
the meanest conception of leisure, ramped
about the land. Montaigne ate and slept
in his unguarded house; read Seneca and

Jacques Amyot; picked up sentences on the vanity of life wherever he could find them, fixing them into the walls of his library; was amiable to his wife and tended his daughter's education, while idealism and turbulence ranged abroad, spilling the wines of France and milk of Burgundy.

For a book to succeed in surviving its own generation is a strange matter. Force, says science, is eternal; but what is force? Calvin lies neglected on the shelf, while Michel de Montaigne prospers and multiplies. His children, the essayists, are like sparrows in spring, singing, chattering, chirping everywhere.

The bed at S—— Point that night was very comfortable. The next day I learned by circuitous questioning — for, I regret to say, I had let my hostess understand, or rather I had not corrected her misunderstanding, that her house had been my hope and aim all the weary afternoon — that I had passed Hulett's in the dark. Post-office, inn, cottages, boathouse, all abed by nine o'clock, and lamps extinguished. Never was there such a pitiful economy of light.

To reach the northern end of the lake

needs but a short paddle. At that point is a little shop, where cider and ginger-pop are sold. The proprietor has a horse and cart, and for a dollar will ferry a canoe across to Lake Champlain. The little river that connects the two lakes is impassable on account of its fall. The mills make a poor return for the turning of their wheels by fouling the water. All the way to Ticonderoga the water looks like slops; there is little pleasure rowing there. I passed the night at Ticonderoga Hotel, and left at dawn. The day began to break as I launched my canoe. Near the shore stood a clump of locust-trees, whose branches interarched, dividing the eastern sky into sections of orange, green, and pink; their trunks black as ink from rain in the night, save on the edges, where the morning colors streaked the outlines with yellow light. In the afternoon of the day before, under the shadow of the trees, I had wondered whether Montaigne had sympathy for the bigger emotions of life. In the early morning I knew that he had not. The rising sun is imperious in its requisition. Under its rays, the blood flows fast, muscles tighten, eyes brighten, cheeks color, sinews swell.

We want love, ambition, recklessness, prayer, fasting, perils, and scars. Talk to us then of

"Le donne, i cavalier, l'arme, gli amori,
Le cortesie, l'audaci imprese."

Keep Seneca and Epictetus for winter evenings, sewing societies, and convalescence. By ill luck it happened that the sun was not an hour high, and the light ran over the ripples on the lake as if creation were beginning, and creation's lord were

"in Werdelust
Schaffender Freude nah,"

when I opened Montaigne and read that he had once been in love. "Je m'y eschauday en mon enfance, et y souffris toutes les rages que les poëtes disent advenir à ceux qui s'y laissent aller sans ordre et sans jugement." "And truly, in my youth I suffered much extremity for love ; very near this." O Montaigne, O Polonius, is your knowledge of life no greater than of these matters ?

Montaigne had a wife who had no part in "toutes les rages." One day, when he was carried home to all appearances dead, he was met by "ceux de ma famille, avec les cris accoustumez en telles choses." He

had children. They died, and he says: "I
lost two or three at nurse, if not without
regret, at least without repining. . . . The
generality of men think it a great blessing
to have many children; I, and some others,
think it as happy to be without them." The
Huguenots give up peace, content, worldly
prosperity, health, and friends for an idea,
and they vex him with their nonconformist
nonsense. Is not Paris worth a mass? Is
not peace more than the absence of branched
candlesticks? The Catholics die for love of
the habit of ages, for tradition, for the divinity in asceticism; and Montaigne *professes*
to be of their faith, *he* too has their religion. He is surrounded by soldiers; what to
him are the big wars, the plumed troops, the
neighing steed, the spirit-stirring drum?

I put Montaigne hastily back under his
blanket and paddled hard, chanting songs of
America. That night I reached Westport.
Lake Champlain is too big for a canoe; it
is so wide that unless you hug the indented
shore you lose the pleasure of an ever shifting scene. The steamboats shake the water
most immoderately. The only way to en-
counter their swell is to meet it bow on, and

lift the boat over the crest of each roll with
a downward stroke of the paddle. At Westport I got aboard the " Chateaugay," and dis-
embarked about noon at a point on the east
side of the lake, opposite Plattsburg. There
I had a very good dinner. It is not far
thence to the border. The lake sluggishly
glides into the river Richelieu. Never was a
less appropriate christening; for a meeker,
duller, feebler river it were hard to imagine.
I had had thoughts of a lively current hurrying me along, but for the life of me I
could not tell which way the river was running. Running, I say, but there was no
more run than Richelieu in this river, except
down a certain rocky declivity, several miles
long, where the water, much against its will,
gives little automatic, jerky jumps, bumping
along till it reaches level again. The first
night on the river I passed at Rouse's Point.
Nothing but Montaigne could have enabled
me to free myself from the oppression of
the dining-room, bedroom, guests, and hotel
clerk. None but Jeremiah could live there.
I had to pay four dollars for the discomforts
of the night. Extortion should be resisted;
but " there is nothing I hate more than driv-

ing of bargaines : it is a meere commerce of
dodging and impudencie. After an hour's
debating and paltring, both parties will goe
from their words and oaths for the getting
or saving of a shilling."

The river Richelieu has its defects and its
virtues. Its chief defect, and a monstrous
one when days are hot and no wind blows,
is that it has no pool, no hollow, no recess,
for a bath. Bushes, lily-pads, water-docks,
and darnels, all manner of slimy herbs range
in unbroken ranks all along the sides. To
take a jump from the canoe in the middle
of the river is a facile feat, "sed revocare
gradum, hic labor est." I poked along for
hours, examining every spot that looked as
if a pebbled bottom might lie underneath,
but found nothing, until I saw a tiny rivulet,
so little that it would take ten minutes to fill
a bathtub, trickling down a bank steeper than
ordinary. Here the oozy greenery parted
respectfully and left an open path for the
little brook to make head into the river.
One step from the shore the bottom sunk
two fathoms deep. I tried to mark the spot
on my map for the sake of future travelers;
but there was no indication of its place; not

even the little house across the river was
noted, the presence of which, perhaps, should
have disturbed me.

The virtues of the Richelieu are those of
the people past whose houses it flows, if those
aggregates of roofs, walls, and chimneys
can be called houses.   In New England a
house implies a family, — father and mother,
children, chickens, and live creatures in general.   These houses have bare existence, no
more.   Not a man is to be seen.   The flat
fields spread far away on either side, and
there are signs of tillage, also pastures tenanted by pigs.   Along the river runs a road,
and at intervals of half a mile little unpainted houses with closed doors and shut
windows stand square-toed upon it.   Once
or twice I saw a woman sewing or knitting
on the doorstep, her back turned; and I
would paddle nearer and strike my paddle a
little more noisily for the sake of a *bonjour*,
or at least of a look with a suggestion of
interest or human curiosity.   The backs remained like so many Ladies of Shalott fearful of consequences.   Perhaps they could
see me in a mirror, perhaps there had been
a time when they used to look; but the river

had been so unremunerative that now no
splash, how noisy soever, could provoke a
turn of the head. It was the land of Nod.
Some children I saw, but voiceless children,
playing drowsy games or sleepily driving
sleeping pigs afield. Bitten with curiosity
and afraid to drink the river's water, I went
up to one of these houses at noontide. I
made a half circle to the back, and found a
door open. In the kitchen sat two women,
an old man, and one or two children; the
women busy sewing, the old man braiding a
mat from long strips of colored cloth. They
all looked up at me and called to the dog,
which had shown more interest in me than
I cared for. One of the defects of the
Richelieu is its dogs. Never were there such
dogs. Dogs by courtesy, for they have legs,
tail, head, ears, and if you go near, they
growl, their hair bristles, and their tails point
stiffly to the ground; but they are not the
dogs honest folks are wont to meet, — mere
gargoyles cast in animated clay. They fetch
their hide from long-haired dogs, Scotch
perhaps, their tails from English bulls, their
throats from hounds, their snouts from point-
ers, their forepaws from dachshunds, their

hind legs from Spitz, their teeth from jackals; their braying, barking, snarling voices are all their own.

"Bonjour," said I, after the dog had lain down. "Voulez-vous avoir la bonté de me donner du lait, madame?" The children stared as before; the women looked at each other, and then at me. I repeated my question, hat in hand. They still stared. "J'ai soif," I continued; "l'eau du fleuve est d'une telle couleur que j'en ai peur." A light broke over the old man's face; one of the women questioned him. "Il veut du lac." "Ah, du lac," and they all smiled, and then clouded up, looking dubious. "Je veux en acheter," said I intelligently. "Ah, il veut en acheter. C'est bien," and the older woman shouted for Jacques. A round-faced young man clambered down a ladder from the attic above the cattle-sheds, and presently brought me some very good milk, with which I filled my pail and departed. As I paddled off I looked back to see who was watching me, making sure that at least a child or the dog would have sufficient curiosity to see the last of me. Not a sign; the house stared indifferently at the water.

I passed one night at St. Johns, which
stands at the southern end of the canal.
The canal runs for twelve miles past the
Chambly Rapids, the same that vexed Samuel
Champlain when he made his first voyage of
discovery, coming down from Mont Real to
punish the Iroquois and to see what he could
see. The lying Algonquins, in their eagerness to have his company, had told him that
there was no obstacle for the canoes. In
this town I lodged in a French inn. The
host was large and portly, — somewhat too
much given to looking like the innkeeper in
Doré's " Don Quixote," but a very good fellow. There is red wine in his cellar, and his
wife cooks omelets with golden-brown tops.

Montaigne is sometimes held up as the
type of the man of the world. It may be
that he is such, but for those of us who are
somewhat abashed at so fine a title, who have
been taught to consider a man of the world
as a hireling of the Prince of this World, and
prefer to cope with a man of our hundred,
the name may carry them into error. It is
true that Montaigne went to Paris while
Catherine de' Medici and her sons held their
court, and to Venice while the fame of Le-

panto still hung over the Adriatic; but he
did not become a man of the world, suppos-
ing that traveling to the worldly cities of the
world can so fashion a man.   He judges
them like a man with a comfortable home in
the country.   " Ces belles villes, Venise et
Paris, alterent la faveur que je leur porte, par
l'aigre senteur, l'une de son marets, l'autre de
sa boue."   In Venice there had been a man
of the world, Pietro Aretino, called *Divine* by
his compatriots, " in whom except it be an
high-raised, proudly pufft, mind-moving and
heart-danting manner of speech, yet in good
sooth more than ordinarie, wittie and ingen-
ious; but so new fangled, so extravagant, so
fantasticall, so deep-laboured ; and to con-
clud, besides the eloquence, which be it as it
may be, I cannot perceive anything in it, beyond or exceeding that of many other writers
of his age, much lesse that it in any sort ap-
proacheth that ancient divinitie."   One sus-
pects that it was not lack of style in Aretino
that repelled Montaigne, but the superabun-
dance of his disgusting nature.   A man of
the world does not have likes and dislikes ;
he has amusements and interests, excitements
even, ennui, tedium, and vacuity.   This aver-

sion from Aretino betrays Montaigne. He
would conceal it as a mere pricking of his
literary thumbs, but the truth will out. There
was not lurking in Montaigne's closet any
skeleton of satiety. That is the mark of the
man of the world. Not abroad, but in his
château, in his study on the third story of
the tower, is Montaigne at his ease. The
world comes to him there, but what world?
This terrestrial globe peopled with ignorance
and knowledge, custom and freedom, "captive good" and "captain ill," where Guise
and Navarre break the peace in all the baili-
wicks of France? By no means. It is Plutarch's world, a novel world of Greeks and
Latins, more like Homer's world than another, where princes and heroes perform
their exploits from some Scamander to the
sea and back again. Plutarch was his encyclopædia of interest. The man of the world
watches the face of the world, walking to
and fro to see what there may be abroad.
Not so Montaigne. He cares little for the
contemporary world of fact, even for the
city of Bordeaux, his charge. Plutarch for
him; and what had Plutarch to do with the
harvests and vintages of Bordeaux, with Gas-

con deaths and Gascon burials, with marriages and children, with drawing water and baking bread, with Ave Marias and Sunday holidays? The heroic, the superhuman, the accomplishment of aspirations and hopes, — these are the domain of Plutarch and also of Romance. Montaigne would not have liked to be dubbed romantic, and clearly he was not; yet the glance and glitter of Romance caught the fancy of this late child of the Renaissance. It is said that the ebb tide of the new birth tumbled him over in its waves and left him lying on the wet sands of disillusion. If this be so, why did he seek and get the citizenship of Rome? Was it not that "Civis Romanus sum" was one of the great permanent realities to his imagination? Why is it that he fills his pages with the romance of Alexander, Scipio, and Socrates? Why do the records of fearlessness facing death, of the stoic suffering the ills of life with a smile, of men doing deeds that surpass the measure of a man's strength, drag him to them? He will not have his heroes belittled. "Moreover, our judgments are but sick, and follow after the corruption of our manners. I see the greater part of the wits

of my time puzzle their brains to draw a
cloud over the glory of the noble and generous feats of old — *grande subtilité*." The
spirit of the Renaissance that wrought by
land and sea in his father's time still lin-
gered. How could a man of letters escape
the spirit of freedom and belief in possibility that the lack of geography and the
babyhood of science spread thick over Europe? To the west lay America and mystery. From the east news might come to-
morrow that the men of Asia were masters
of Vienna. From the spire of Bordeaux
Cathedral a mayor standing a-tiptoe might
see the cut of Drake's jib as he sailed up
the Gironde. Romance impregnated the air.
Into France, reformation, classic lore, the
arts of Italy, were come at double-quick, and
to the south, in a certain place in La Mancha,
El Señor Quixada, or Quesada, gave himself
over to reading books of knight-errantry
with so much zeal that he clean forgot to
go a-hunting, and even to attend to his property; in fact, this gentleman's curiosity and
nonsense in this matter reached such a pitch
that he sold many an acre of cornfields in
order to buy books of knight-errantry. Mon-

taigne had too much of Polonius to behave
in that way ; nevertheless, the desire to reach
out beyond the chalk - line drawn by the
senses was potent with him. He goes round
and round a subject not merely to show how
no progress can be made towards discover-
ing the inner reality of it, but partly to see
if he cannot discover something. The make-
weights that kept him steadfast in sobriety
were his curiosity and his wit. Wit is the
spirit that ties a man's leg. It cannot abide
half-lights, shadows, and darkness. Wit must
deal with the immediate, with the plat of
ground round which it paces its intellectual
circuit. Wit has a lanthorn, which sheds
its beams, revealing unexpected knowledge,
but it turns the twilight beyond that circle
of light into darkness. Ariosto's wit makes
his verses, but bars him from poetry. Spenser's lack of wit allows him to make poetry,
but shuts him out from readers. Shakespeare and Cervantes were great enough to
dominate their wit, but Montaigne's clasped
hands with his curiosity, and the two led him
as the dog leads a blind man. The instinct
in them has guided him to immortality. In
curiosity Montaigne was of his father's time.

Curiosity was one of the makers of the Renaissance. It has not the graces of resignation and of contemplation, it lacks the self-respect of belief and the self-sufficiency of unbelief, but it accomplishes more than they, it must be reckoned with. It is the force underlying science. It is the grand vizier of change. Curiosity whispered to Columbus, plucked Galileo by the sleeve, and shook the apple off Newton's apple-tree. Montaigne was a curious man. The English language lacks nicety in not having two words for the two halves of curiosity : one for Francis Bacon, one for my landlady's neighbor, she that lives behind us to the left, whose window commands our yard. But if there were, could we apply the nobler adjective to Montaigne? Does he want to *know*, like Ulysses? Will he to ocean in an open boat,

> " yearning in desire
> To follow knowledge like a sinking star " ?

Or does he rest content with the ordinary wares of knowledge, sold in market overt, and is he satisfied with ruminating over them, hands in pockets, leaving others to buy and use?

The placidity of his life is another proof

of his fondness for romance. A man of the world must go out into the world to seek the motion and the tap-tap of the free play of life, in order to satisfy the physical needs of sight and sound. The man of imagination and romance sits in his study, and heroes, heroines, gryphons, and Ganelons come huddling about his chair. To Montaigne the world came through his books, yet he is not a representative scholar. His companionship with books is based on friendship, not on desire for knowledge. There is no latent Faust in him. He is a man of the library. Of all great men of letters, more than the rest he has his writing-table backgrounded and shut in by bookshelves. Cicero is a man of the forum, Voltaire of the theatre, Walter Scott of hill and dale. Montaigne is at home with books, not with men. Of the former, his cronies are Plutarch, Seneca, Cicero, Horace. He cares not so much about states and policies as he does how states long dead and policies forgotten appear to philosopher and poet. He is indifferent to morals as affecting the happiness of men, and eagerly interested in them as a topic of conversation, as an occasion whereby opinion may take

the foils against opinion, and thought click
against its fellow. Nor is he fond of poetry
except as it serves to embroider his mono-
logues. Life itself interests him chiefly as a
matter for talk. And how good his talk is,
how excellent his speech! With his heart,
or what of heart he had, in his books, it
is natural that he wished to appear among
men of letters in his best array. He was
ambitious, when men thenceforward should
read Cicero and Seneca, that Michel de Montaigne should be read too, and that his style
should stand beside theirs, uncovered, *par
inter pares.* Sainte-Beuve, making mention
of Calvin, Rabelais, Pascal, and Montaigne,
says that Rabelais and Montaigne are poets.
But Montaigne clearly does not fill an English-speaking man's conception of a poet. It
must be, I think, that Sainte-Beuve was under the influence of Montaigne's language,
and therefore called him so. That was natural. The French tongue at that time had
a strong element of poetry; it bore deep
marks of its originals. It had not yet come
under the complete dominion of narrow pros-
ody and syntax. The words had in a measure the simplicity, the indecision of outline,

the rude strength, of the Teutonic languages. Old English words, at times, like conspirators, come fraught with greater meaning that they are indistinct; their shadows fall about them, hiding their feet; they glide into your presence : so it is with Montaigne's words. Nowadays French words have evolutions and drills, accepted manœuvres; they savor of mathematics and bloodless things. The French language of to-day has altered its sixteenth-century habit more than English has ; no Bible arrested its development. Montaigne has the simplicity, the directness of expression and exposition, of the men of to-day, but the poetical quality that lurks in his words and phrases they have not inherited.

At St. Johns is the custom house, but the office was locked at a reasonable hour in the morning for calling, and I felt under no further obligations towards the Canadian government. Here also is the place to pay the canal toll, and in exchange receive a ticket which gives permission to pass all the locks. The toll-taker wrote me out a permit, full of dignity, authorizing the ship Sickle-Fin, weighing not more than one ton, whereof

Captain ——, naming me, was the master, laden with ballast (Montaigne), to travel free through all the locks.

It is the every-day humanity in Montaigne that binds us to him. It is his lack of capacity for self-sacrifice, his inability to believe, his ignorance of love, his innocence of scorn. These are our common property. He likes the comforts that we like ; he values security, ease, simplicity, a fire on the hearth, a book in the hand, fresh water in summer. He never makes us ashamed.

The next night I passed at Belœil. Here I was the sport of indecision for an hour, unable to make up my mind where to pass the night. There were three hotels, two on my left, one on my right. While looking at each in turn, I resolved to go to one of the other two. Finally I made my choice. I selected a little wooden house, with a little bar-room, a little dining-room, and a very tiny larder, and beer of a despicable quality. I had ham and eggs for dinner, — " Si l'on avait su que Monsieur allait venir, on aurait pu avoir un bifteck," — ham and eggs for breakfast, and an offer to put up ham and eggs for my lunch.

The villages along the river are all on one pattern. In the centre is a very large church, so big that you see it far off, long before there is any other indication of human life. The church is built on a rectangle, with a pointed roof and a tall spire tipped with a weather-cock. The roof is covered with tin, unpainted, which does not rust, perhaps because the air is so dry, and flashes very gaudily in the sun. Grouped about the church are large red brick buildings facing a little green. These are the houses for priests and nuns, with the offices for parish work. Images of the Virgin and saints stand about. The grass-plot and the paths are well kept, and were it not that the rest of the village does not seem to share in this prosperity, it would be a very pleasant sight. At St. Ours, where I passed the next night, there was an attractive house, shut in by a garden and well protected by trees, that had the look of accumulated savings; but in general there was little sign of the comforts so often seen in the small manufacturing villages of New England, — no sound of a lawn-mower, no croquet, no tennis.

The river Richelieu joins the St. Lawrence at Sorel. There I found that the St. Lawrence is too big and strong for a canoe, at least when paddled in a jogging, unsophisticated way. I put my canoe aboard the steamer, and bought a ticket for Quebec. In my stuffy cabin, under the dim gaslight, I admired Montaigne's imperturbability and his ceaseless interest in things.

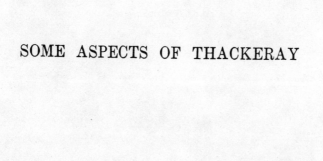

SOME ASPECTS OF THACKERAY

SOME ASPECTS OF THACKERAY

I

TWENTY years ago, at Harvard College, in the rooms of all students of certain social pretensions who affected books, you were sure to see on the most conspicuous shelf, in green and gold or in half calf, the works of William Makepeace Thackeray. The name, boldly printed, greeted you as you entered the door, and served, together with sundry red-sealed certificates and beribboned silver medals, to inform you of the general respectability and gentility of your host. Of a Sunday morning, this student was likely to be discovered complacent over the "Book of Snobs" or serious over "Vanity Fair."

Public opinion went that Thackeray was the novelist of gentlemen and for gentlemen; that Dickens was undoubtedly strong, but he had not had the privilege of knowing and of delineating the things which were adapted to interest the most select of Harvard undergraduates. In every fold there are some to lower the general standard of critical excellence; there were some partisans of Dickens. They were judged, as minorities are, found guilty of running counter to accepted opinions, and outlawed from further literary criticism.

These Harvard critics did not make for themselves this opinion of Thackeray; they brought it with them from home.

We suppose that parents, what time their son started in the world on the first path which diverged from theirs, deemed that they were equipping him with the best master to teach him concerning the ways of that world. Theirs was the old lack of faith, so common to the fearful; they sought to guard their son from the world by pointing out to him its vanity, its folly, its emptiness. "Oh, if he shall only know what the world is," they thought, "he will escape its evils to come." So they gave him Thackeray, and wrote him long letters on idleness and vice. His bookshelves and his inner pockets thus encumbered, the youth found Harvard College a miniature of the world of which he had been warned. There were materials

enough for such a conclusion. A seeker
will find what he goes forth to seek. The
youth learned his Thackeray well, spent four
years enjoying his little Vanity Fair, and
then departed from Cambridge to help build
up the larger world of Vanity which shows so
fine in America to-day.

There is no phenomenon so interesting as
the unconscious labor of boys and men over
the task of shaping, hewing, whittling, and
moulding the world into accord with their
anticipations. All lend helping hands to the
great master implement, public expectation.
A young fellow goes to college, and joins a
group of a dozen others. Brown, the rake,
thinks, "Here's a Lothario who will sup at
Dame Quickly's with me;" Smith, the boxer,
says, "A quick eye, — I'll make a boxer of
him;" Jones, who translates Homer for the
group, sees rhythm and Theocritus in the
newcomer's curly hair; Robinson, the philosopher, feels a fellow Hegelian. These
rival expectations leap out to meet the stran-
ger; they struggle among themselves. Of
the students, some agree with Brown, some
with Smith, others with Robinson or Jones.
The sturdiest of these expectations chokes

out the others and survives. After a short
time — our young fellow yet entirely undis-
covered — a strong current of unanimous
expectation has decided that he shall be a
boxer. All obstacles to the execution of this
judgment are taken away, and moral earth-
works are quickly thrown up, guarding him
from Brown, Jones, and Robinson. Expectation seats him beside Smith ; expectation
turns the conversation upon champions of
the ring ; expectation draws the gloves upon
his fists; it offers him no Eastcheap, no
Theocritus, no Hegel. The youth takes box-
ing lessons ; soon he learns the language of
the fraternity ; he walks, runs, avoids mince
pies, eschews books, and with a single eye
looks forward to a bout in Hemenway Gym-
nasium. Thus the tricksy spirit expectation
shapes the destinies of common humankind.
Thus do parents begin to expect that their son
will see the world with their own and Thackeray's beam-troubled eyes ; they insist that
he shall, and in due time he does.

Once convince a young man that Thackeray's world is the real world, that vulgarity,
meanness, trickery, and fraud abound, and
you put him in a yoke from which he shall

never free himself. This is the yoke of base
expectation. This is what is known in Scrip-
ture as " the world ; " it is the habit of screw-
ing up the eyes and squinting in order to see
unworthiness, baseness, vice, and wickedness ;
it is a creeping blindness to nobler things.
The weapon against the world is, as of old,
to use a word of great associations, faith.
Faith is nothing but noble expectation, and
all education should be to supplant base expectation by noble expectation. What is the
human world in which we live but a mighty
mass of sensitive matter, highly susceptible
to the great force of human expectation,
which flows about it like an ever shifting
Gulf Stream, now warming and prospering
noble people, and then wantonly comforting
the unworthy ?

Feeble folk that we are, we have in this
power of creation an element of divinity in
us. Our expectations hover about like life-
giving agencies. We are conscious that our
hopes and our fears are at work all the time
helping the oncoming of that which we hope
or fear. The future is like a new born babe
stretching out its arms to the stronger. It
may be that this power in us is weak, inter-

mittent, often pitiably feeble ; but now and again comes a man with a larger measure of divine life, and his great expectations pass into deeds. Before every Trafalgar first comes an expectation that duty will be done.

Thackeray has no faith ; he does not entertain high expectations. His characters do shameless things, and Thackeray says to the reader, " Be not surprised, injured-seeming friend ; you would have done the like under the like temptation." At first you contradict, you resent ; but little by little Thackeray's opinion of you inoculates you ; the virus takes ; you lose your conviction that you would have acted differently ; you concede that such conduct was not impossible, even for you, — no, nor improbable, — and, on the whole, after reflection, that the conduct was excusable, was good enough, was justified, was inevitable, was right, was scrupulously right, and only a Don Quixote would have acted otherwise.

Nothing sickens and dies so quickly as noble expectation. Luxury, comfort, custom, the ennui of hourly exertion, the dint of disappointment, assail it unceasingly : if a man of ten talents, like Thackeray, joins the assailants, is it not just that admiration of him should be confined to those who are willing to admire talents, irrespective of the use to which they are put ?

II

England has found it hard to bring forth men of faith. In the great days of Queen Elizabeth, a number of uniting causes produced an emotional excitement which lifted Englishmen and Englishwomen to such a height that Shakespeare saw Othello, Hamlet, Brutus, Coriolanus, Miranda, Cordelia. There was the material stimulus of commerce with strange countries, the prick of money ; there was this curious earth, inviting wooers ; there was the goad of conscience, troubled to renounce the religion of old ; there was the danger of foreign conquerors ; there was manly devotion to a Virgin Queen. England roused herself, and, " like a dewdrop from the lion's mane," shook off the trammels of petty interests, of vulgar self-seeking, and presented to her poet great sights of human nobility. Not that the moral elevation of a nation is very much higher at one time than at another, but a

little swelling of noble desires so breaks
the ice of custom that a poet must see the
clearer waters which lie beneath. If Shakespeare were alive to-day, we doubt not that
he would tell of new Othellos, new Cordelias;
but it was easier for him then than it would
be now, or how could such a host of noble
men and women people his pages?

Since that time England has been prosperous and comfortable ; and as her comfort
and prosperity have increased she has drifted
further and further from a great acceptance
of the world. Dryden and his group, Fielding, Sheridan, men of talents in their different generations, have succeeded, who contemplate themselves, and, expecting to find
the world a fit place for them to live in, have
helped to render it so.

A hundred years ago England shook herself free from the dominion of vulgar men.
In France, the triple burden of church, mon-
arch, and nobility, the prohibition of thought,
the injustice of power, had lain like mill-
stones on the people ; each individual had
borne his own burden, but one after another
each saw that not he alone groaned and
sweated, but his brothers also. The fardel a

man can bear by himself he can no longer
carry when he sees an endless line of other
men weighted down and staggering. Sight
of injustice to others made each individual in
France throw off his own yoke; and the most
exultant cry of justice, of brotherly love, ever
heard, was raised. No country lives alone.
French passion flushed to England. Englishmen were roused : some were for liberty ;
others saw their dull old homes and habits
transfigured in the blaze of new ideas. Noble
Republicans bred noble Tories. Everything
was ennobled ; babies looked more beautiful to
their mothers ; Virgil interested schoolboys ;
ragamuffins and ploughboys felt strange dis-
quiet as they heard the words " liberty,"
" country," " brotherhood," " home." This
shock and counter-shock prepared the way for
the great poets of that time, and made Walter Scott possible. Scott had faith ; he saw
a noble world. But the idealism of France
passed away, its glow faded from the English
cliffs ; danger was locked up in St. Helena,
and prosperity and comfort, like Gog and
Magog, stalked through England.

Thackeray was bred when Englishmen
were forsaking " swords for ledgers," and de-

serting " the student's bower for gold." His
father died when he was very young. His
mother married for her second husband an
Indian officer, and Thackeray was sent to
school in England.

In a new biographical edition of Thackeray's works which Messrs. Harper & Brothers
are publishing, Mrs. Ritchie has written brief
memories of her father at the beginning of
each volume, with special relation to its contents. These memories are done with filial
affection. Thackeray's kindness, his tenderness, his sympathetic nature, are written large
on every page. He has many virtues. He
dislikes vice, drunkenness, betrayal of women,
pettifogging, huckstering, lying, cheating,
knavery, the annoyance and tomfoolery of
social distinctions. He would like to leave
the world better than he found it, but
he cannot see. Pettiness, the vulgarity of
money, the admiration of mean things, hang
before him like a curtain at the theatre. Ro-
meo may be on fire, Hotspur leap for the
moon, Othello stab Iago, Lear die in Cordelia's lap ; but the sixteenth of an inch of
frieze and fustian keeps it all from him.

At nineteen Thackeray spent a winter at

Weimar.   He soon writes to his mother of
Goethe as " the great lion of Weimar."   He
is not eager to possess the great measures of
life.   He is not sensitive to Goethe, but to
the court of Pumpernickel.   He wishes he
were a cornet in Sir John Kennaway's yeomanry, that he might wear the yeoman's
dress.   " A yeomanry dress is always a hand-
some and respectable one."

In 1838, when in Paris, he writes : " I have
just come from seeing ' Marion Delorme,' the
tragedy of Victor Hugo, and am so sickened
and disgusted with the horrid piece that I
have hardly heart to write."   He did not
look through pain and extravagance into the
noble passion of the play.   He lived in a
moral Pumpernickel where the ideal is kept
outside the town gates.   And he has described his home with the vividness and
vigor of complete comprehension.   Never
has a period had so accomplished an historian.   The *bourgeoisie* have their epic in
" Vanity Fair."

This book reflects Thackeray's intellectual
image in his prime ; it is his first great novel,
and is filled with the most vivid and enduring
of his beliefs and convictions.   There are in

it a vigor, an independence, and a sense of
power that come when a man faces his best
opportunity.   Into it Thackeray has put what
he deemed the truest experiences of his life.
" The Newcomes " and " Pendennis " are but
sequels.   " The Newcomes " is the story of
his stepfather, in Vanity Fair; " Pendennis,"
that of Thackeray himself and his mother
wandering in its outskirts.   There is this
one family of nice people, gathered into an
ark as it were, floating over the muddy waters.   Thackeray was able to see that his
immediate family were not rogues ; he was
also able to draw a most noble gentleman,
Henry Esmond, by the help of the idealizing
lens of a hundred odd years; but the world
he thought he saw about him is the world
of " Vanity Fair."

Thackeray had so many fine qualities that
one cannot but feel badly to see him in such
a place.   Had his virtues — his kindness,
his tenderness, his charm, his capacity for
affection — been energetic enough to dominate his entire character, he would have lived
among far different scenes ; his readers would
have beheld him brooding over a world where
passion may be very noble and very base,

happy that virtue, in the strong or in the weak, may sometimes be found indomitable, and deeply serious, deeply conscious of that inner essence in men, which at times has persuaded them to believe themselves children of God. Was it Thackeray's fault that this was not to be? Or did he suffer the incidental misfortunes which large causes bring to individuals as they follow their own regardless paths?

III

Thackeray is the poet of respectability. His working time stretches from the Reform Act almost to the death of Lord Palmerston. He chronicles the contemporary life of a rich, money-getting generation of merchants and manufacturers, lifted into sudden importance in the national life by steamboats and railroads, by machinery for spinning, weaving, mining, by Arkwright, Watt, Davy, and Stephenson. His is a positive, matter-of-fact world, of which Peel is the statesman and Macaulay the man of letters. Macaulay, in his essay on Bacon, has given us the measure of its spiritual elevation : "We have sometimes thought that an amusing fiction

might be written, in which a disciple of Epictetus and a disciple of Bacon should be introduced as fellow travelers. They come to
a village where the smallpox has just begun
to rage, and find houses shut up, intercourse
suspended, the sick abandoned, mothers
weeping in terror over their children. The
Stoic assures the dismayed population that
there is nothing bad in the smallpox; and
that, to a wise man, disease, deformity, death,
the loss of friends, are not evils. The Baconian takes out a lancet and begins to vac-
cinate. They find a body of miners in great
dismay. An explosion of noisome vapors
has just killed many of those who were at
work; and the survivors are afraid to ven-
ture into the cavern. The Stoic assures them
that such an accident is nothing but a mere
ἀποπροήγμενον. The Baconian, who has
no such fine word at his command, contents
himself with devising a safety-lamp. They
find a shipwrecked merchant wringing his
hands on the shore. His vessel, with an in-
estimable cargo, has just gone down, and he
is reduced in a moment from opulence to
beggary. The Stoic exhorts him not to seek
happiness in things which lie without him-

self ; the Baconian constructs a diving-bell.
It would be easy to multiply illustrations of
the difference between the philosophy of
thorns and the philosophy of fruit, the philosophy of words and the philosophy of
works." This is the very nobility of machinery. As we read, we listen to the buzz
and whirr of wheels, the drip of oil-cans, the
creaking and straining of muscle and steel.
Such things serve, no doubt, in default of
other agencies, to create a great empire, but
the England of Thackeray's day was *nouveau
riche*, self-made, proud of its lack of occupation other than money-getting.

During the formative period of Thackeray's life the English nation was passing
under the influence of machinery. There
was the opportunity of a great man of letters, such as Thackeray, to look to it that
literature should respond to the stimulus of
added power, and grow so potent that it
would determine what direction the national
life should take. At such a time of national
expansion, literature should have seen England in the flush of coming greatness ; it
should have roused itself to re-create her in
nobler imagination, and have spent itself in

making her accept this estimate and expectation, and become an England dominating material advantages and leading the world.

The interest in life is this potentiality and malleability. The allotted task of men and women is to take this potentiality and shape it. Men who have strong intelligence and quick perceptions, like Thackeray, accomplish a great deal in the way of giving a definite form to the material with which life furnishes us. What Michelangelo says of marble is true of life : —

> " Non ha l'ottimo artista alcun concetto
> Ch'un marmo solo in se non circoscriva
> Col suo soverchio."

The problem of life is to uncover the figures hiding in this material : shall it be Caliban and Circe, or Philip Sidney and Jeanne d'Arc ? Thackeray, with what Mrs. Ritchie calls " his great deal of common sense," saw Major Pendennis and Becky Sharp ; and he gave more effective cuttings and chiselings and form to the potential life of England than any other man of his time.

The common apology for such a novelist is that he describes what he sees. This is the worst with which we charge him. We

charge Thackeray with seeing what he describes; and what justification has a man, in
a world like this, to spend his time looking
at Barnes Newcome and Sir Pitt Crawley?
Thackeray takes the motes and beams floating in his mind's eye for men and women,
writes about them, and calls his tale a history.

Thackeray wrote, on finishing "Vanity
Fair," that all the characters were odious
except Dobbin. Poor Thackeray, what a
world to see all about him, with his tender,
affectionate nature! Even Colonel Newcome is so crowded round by a mob of ras-
cally fellows that it is hard to do justice to
Thackeray's noblest attempt to be a poet.
But why see a world, and train children to
see a world, where

"The great man is a vulgar clown"?

A world with such an unreal standard must
be an unreal world. In the real world vulgar clowns are not great men. Thackeray
sees a world all topsy-turvy, and it does not
occur to him that he, and not the world, is
at fault. This is the curse of faithlessness.
He himself says, "The world is a looking-

glass, and gives back to every man the reflection of his own face."

Thackeray has been praised as a master of reality. As reality is beyond our ken, the phrase is unfortunate; but the significance of it is that if a man will portray to the mob the world with which the mob is familiar, they will huzza themselves hoarse. Has not the Parisian mob shouted for Zola? Do not the Madrileños cheer Valdés? Do not Ouida and the pale youth of Rome and Paris holla, " d'Annunzio! d'Annunzio! " There is no glory here. The poet, not in fine frenzy, but in sober simplicity, tells the mob, not what they see, but what they cannot of themselves perceive, with such a tone of authority that they stand gaping and likewise see.

Thackeray's love of reality was merely an embodiment of the popular feeling which proposed to be direct, business-like, and not to tolerate any nonsense. People felt that a money-getting country must take itself seriously. The Reform Act had brought political control to the bourgeoisie, men of common sense; no ranters, no will-o'-the-wisp chasers, but "burgomasters and great oneyers,"—men who thought very highly of circumstances under which they were prosperous, and asked for no more beautiful sight than their own virtues. Influenced by the sympathetic touch of this atmosphere, novel-readers found their former favorites old-fashioned. Disraeli, Samuel Warren, Bulwer Lytton, G. P. R. James, seemed false, theatrical, and sentimental. Thackeray was of this opinion, and he studied the art of caricature as the surest means of saving himself from any such fantastic nonsense. He approached life as a city man, — one who was convinced that the factories of London, not the theories of the philosopher, were the real motive force underneath all the busy flow of outward life. He found his talents exactly suited to this point of view. His memory was an enormous wallet, into which his hundred-handed observation was day and night tossing scraps and bits of daily experience. He saw the meetings of men as he passed : lords, merchants, tinsmiths, guardsmen, tailors, cooks, valets, nurses, policemen, boys, applewomen, — everybody whom you meet of a morning between your house and your office in the city. He remarked the gestures, he heard the words, he guessed what had gone before, he divined what would happen thereafter : and each sight, sound, guess, and divination was safely stowed away.   England of the forties, as Thackeray saw it, is in " Vanity Fair," " Pendennis," and " The Newcomes."   " I ask you to believe," he says in the preface to " Pendennis," " that this person writing strives to tell the truth."

Where lies the truth ?   Are men merely outward parts of machinery, exposed to view, while down below in the engine-room steam and electricity determine their movements? Or do men live and carry on their daily routine under the influence of some great thought of which they are half unconscious, but by which they are shaped, moulded, and moved ?   A French poet says : —

" Le vrai Dieu, le Dieu fort, est le Dieu des idées."

But Macaulay says that the philosophy of Plato began with words and ended with words ; that an acre in Middlesex is better than a principality in Utopia.   The British public applauded Macaulay, and young Thackeray took the hint.

IV

Nobody can question Thackeray's style.
His fame is proof of its excellence. Even if
a man will flatter the mob by saying that he
sees what they see, he cannot succeed without skill of expression. Readers are slow
to understand. They need grace, pithy sentences, witty turns of phrase, calculated sweep
of periods and paragraphs. They must have
no labor of attention; the right adjective
alone will catch their eyes; they require
their pages plain, clear, perspicuous. In all
these qualities Thackeray is very nearly perfect. Hardly anybody would say that there
is a novel better written than " Vanity Fair."
The story runs as easily as the hours. Chapter after chapter in the best prose carries the
reader comfortably on. Probably this excellence is due to Thackeray's great powers of
observation. His eyes saw everything, saving for the blindness of his inward eye, and
his memory held it. He was exceedingly
sensitive. Page after page is filled with the
vividness of well-chosen detail. He cultivated the art of writing most assiduously.
From 1830 to 1847, when " Vanity Fair,"

the first of his great novels, was published,
he was writing all the time, and for almost
all of that time as a humorist, drawing cari-
catures, — a kind of writing perhaps better
adapted than any other to cultivate the power
of portraying scenes. The caricaturist is re-
stricted to a few lines; his task does not
allow him to fill in, to amplify; he must say
his say in little. The success of wit is the
arrangement of a dozen words. This training
for sixteen continuous years taught Thackeray a style which, for his subjects, has no
equal in English literature.

To-day we greatly admire Stevenson and
Kipling. We applaud Stevenson's style for
its cultivation and its charm; we heap praises
upon Kipling's for its dash, vigor, and accuracy of detail. All these praises are deserved;
but when we take up Thackeray again, we
find pages and pages written in a style
more cultivated than Stevenson's and equally
charming, and with a dash, vigor, and nicety
of detail that Kipling might envy. Descriptions that would constitute the bulk of an
essay for the one, or of a story for the other,
do hasty service as prologues to Thackeray's
chapters. Conversations of a happy theatri-

cal turn, with enough exaggeration to appear
wholly natural, which Stevenson and Kipling
never have rivaled, come crowding together
in his long novels.

There are two famous scenes which are
good examples of Thackeray's power, — one
of his sentiment, one of his humor. The first
is Colonel Newcome's death in the Charter-
house. The second is the first scene between
Pendennis and the Fotheringay. " Pen tried
to engage her in conversation about poetry
and about her profession. He asked her
what she thought of Ophelia's madness, and
whether she was in love with Hamlet or not.
' In love with such a little ojus wretch as that
stunted manager of a Bingley ? ' She bris-
tled with indignation at the thought. Pen
explained it was not of her he spoke, but
of Ophelia of the play. ' Oh, indeed ; if no
offense was meant, none was taken : but as
for Bingley, indeed, she did not value him,
— not that glass of punch.' Pen next tried
her on Kotzebue. ' Kotzebue ? Who was
he ? ' ' The author of the play in which she
had been performing so admirably.' ' She
did not know that — the man's name at the
beginning of the book was Thompson,' she

said. Pen laughed at her adorable simplicity. He told her of the melancholy fate
of the author of the play, and how Sand had
killed him. . . . 'How beautiful she is!'
thought Pen, cantering homewards. 'How
simple and how tender! How charming it
is to see a woman of her genius busying herself with the humble offices of domestic life,
cooking dishes to make her old father comfortable, and brewing him drink! How rude
it was of me to begin to talk about profes-
sional matters, and how well she turned the
conversation! . . . Pendennis, Pendennis, —
how she spoke the word! Emily, Emily! how
good, how noble, how beautiful, how perfect,
she is!'"

This scene is very close upon farce, and it
is in that borderland that Thackeray's extraordinary skill shows itself most conspicuous. Difficult, however, as it must be to be
a master there, — and the fact that Thackeray has no rival in this respect proves it, —
it is easy work compared to drawing a scene
of real love, of passion. Perhaps some actions of Lady Castlewood are Thackeray's
only attempt thereat. The world of passion
is not his world. His ear is not attuned to

"Das tiefe, schmerzenvolle Glück
Des Hasses Kraft, die Macht der Liebe."

Charlotte Brontë, Tourguenef, Hawthorne, Hugo, Balzac, all excel him. Thackeray hears the click of custom against custom, the throb of habit, the tick-tick of vulgar life, all the sounds of English social machinery. What interests him is the relation that Harry Foker or Blanche Amory bears to the standard of social excellence accepted by commercial England in the forties. He is never — at least as an artist — disturbed by any scheme of metaphysics. His English common sense is never lured afield by any speculations about the value of a human being uncolored by the shadows of time and space. He is never troubled by doubts of standards, by skepticism as to uses, ends, purposes ; he has a hard-and-fast British standard. He draws Colonel Newcome as an object of pity ; he surrounds him with tenderness and sympathy. Here is Thackeray at his highest. But he never suggests to the reader that Colonel Newcome is not a man to be pitied, but to be envied ; not a failure, but a success ; not unhappy, but most fortunate. The great poets of the world have turned the malefactor's cross into the symbol of holiness. Thackeray never departs from the British middle class conceptions of triumph and failure. In all his numerous dissertations and asides to the reader, he wrote like the stalwart Briton he was, good, generous, moral, domestic, stern, and tender. You never forget his Puritan ancestry, you can rely upon his honesty; but he is not pureminded or humble. He dislikes wrong, but he never has a high enough conception of right to hate wrong. His view is that it is a matter to be cured by policemen, propriety, and satire.

Satire is the weapon of the man at odds with the world and at ease with himself. The dissatisfied man — a Juvenal, a Swift, a youthful Thackeray — belabors the world with vociferous indignation, like the wind on the traveler's back, the beating makes it hug its cloaking sins the tighter. Wrong runs no danger from such chastisement. The fight against wrong is made by the man discontented with himself and careless of the world. Satire is harmless as a moral weapon. It is an old-fashioned fowling piece, fit for a man of wit, intelligence, and a certain limited

imagination. It runs no risk of having no
quarry; the world to it is one vast covert of
lawful game. It goes a-traveling with wit,
because both are in search of the unworthy.
It is well suited to a brilliant style. It is
also a conventional department in literature,
and as such is demanded by publishers and
accepted by the public.

Thackeray was born with dexterity of observation, nimbleness of wit, and a quick
sense of the incongruous and the grotesque.
He lost his fortune when a young man. He
wrote for a livelihood, and naturally turned
to that branch of literature which was best
suited to his talents. It was his misfortune
that satire is bad for a man's moral development. It intensified his natural disbelief in
the worth of humanity, but gave him the
schooling that enabled him to use his powers
so brilliantly.

Thackeray was often hampered by this
habit of looking at the grotesque side of
things. It continually dragged him into
farce, causing feebleness of effect where there
should have been power. Sir Pitt Crawley,
Jos Sedley, the struggle over Miss Crawley,
Harry Foker, the Chevalier de Florac, Aunt

Hoggerty, are all in the realm of farce. This is due partly to Thackeray's training, and partly to his attitude toward life. If life consists of money, clothes, and a bundle of social relations, our daily gravity, determination, and vigor are farcical, because they are so out of place; they are as incongruous as a fish in trousers. But Thackeray forgets that there is something disagreeable in this farce, as there would be in looking into Circe's sty and seeing men groveling over broken meats. To be sure, Thackeray makes believe that he finds it comic to see creatures of great pretensions busy themselves so continually with the pettiest things. But it too often seems as if the comic element consisted in our human pretensions, and as if Thackeray merely kept bringing them to the reader's notice for the sake of heightening the contrast between men and their doings.

V

Thackeray is not an innovator; he follows the traditions of English literature. He is in direct descent from the men of the "Spectator," Addison, Steele, and their friends, and from Fielding. He has far greater powers

of observation, wit, humor, sentiment, and
description than the "Spectator" group. He
excels Fielding in everything except as a
story-teller, and in a kind of intellectual
power that is more easily discerned in Fielding than described, — a kind of imperious
understanding that breaks down a path before it, whereas Thackeray's intelligence
looks in at a window or peeps through the
keyhole.   Fielding is the bigger, coarser
man of the two; Thackeray is the cleverer.
Each is thoroughly English.   Fielding embodies the England of George I.; Thackeray, that same England refined by the re-
volutionary ideas of 1789, trained by long
wars, then materialized by machinery, by a
successful bourgeoisie, and the quick acces-
sion of wealth.   Each is a good fellow, —
quick in receiving ideas, but slow to learn a
new point of view.   Fielding is inferior to
Thackeray in education, in experience of
many men, and in foreign travel.   Tom
Jones is the begetter of Arthur Pendennis,
Jonathan Wild of Barry Lyndon.   Some of
Fielding's heroines, wandering out of " Tom
Jones " and " Amelia," have strayed into
" Pendennis," " Vanity Fair," and " The

Newcomes." The fair émigrées change their
names, but keep their thoughts and behavior.

It is said that a lady once asked Thackeray why he made all his women fools or
knaves. "Madam, I know no others." It
may be that living in Paris in his youth hurt
his insight into women; it may be that the
great sorrow of his wife's insanity instinc-
tively turned his thoughts from the higher
types of women; perhaps his life in Bohemia
and in clubs limited his knowledge during
the years when novel-writing was his chief
occupation. The truth seems to be that
Thackeray, like Fielding, was a man's man,
— he understood one cross-section of a common man, his hopes, aims, fears, wishes,
habits, and manners; but he was very ignorant of women. He says: "Desdemona was
not angry with Cassio, though there is very
little doubt she saw the lieutenant's partiality for her (and I, for my part, believe that
many more things took place in that sad
affair than the worthy Moorish officer ever
knew of); why, Miranda was even very kind
to Caliban, and we may be pretty sure for
the same reason. Not that she would en-

courage him in the least, the poor uncouth monster, — of course not." Shakespeare and Thackeray looked differently at women.

Thackeray lacked the poet's eye; he could not see and was not troubled.

> " Ahi quanto nella mente mi commossi,
>   Quando mi volsi per veder Beatrice,
>   Per non poter vedere, ben ch'io fossi
> Presso di lei, e nel mondo felice ! "

But poor Thackeray was never near the ideal, and never in paradise. Some critic has said of him that because he had Eden in his mind's eye, this world appeared a Vanity Fair. No criticism could be more perverted; he had Vanity Fair in his mind's eye, and therefore could not see paradise.

This treatment of women is half from sheer ignorance, and half from Thackeray's habit of dealing in caricature with subjects of which he is ignorant. He behaves toward foreign countries very much as he does toward women. France, Germany, Italy, appear like geography in an opera bouffe. They are places for English blackguards to go to, and very fit places for them, tenanted as they are by natives clad in outlandish trousers, and bearded and mustachioed like

pards. Of the French he says : "In their
aptitude to swallow, to utter, to enact hum-
bugs, these French people, from Majesty
downwards, beat all the other nations of
this earth. In looking at these men, their
manners, dresses, opinions, politics, actions,
history, it is impossible to preserve a grave
countenance ; instead of having Carlyle to
write a history of the French Revolution, I
often think it should be handed over to Dickens or Theodore Hook. . . . I can hardly
bring my mind to fancy that anything is
serious in France, — it seems to be all rant,
tinsel, and stage-play." His attitude toward
French literature is distorted by lack of sympathy to an astonishing degree.

Thackeray's fault was not merely a certain
narrowness of mind, but also that he allowed
himself to see only the grotesque and disagreeable, until habit and nature combined to
blind him to other things.

VI

Thackeray is not a democrat. Democracy,
like many another great and vague social
conception, is based upon a fundamental
truth, of which its adherents are often igno-

rant, although they brush against it in the dark and unwittingly draw in strength for their belief. The fundamental truth of democracy is that the real pleasures of life are increased by sharing them, — that exclusiveness renders pleasure insipid. One reason why democracy has prevailed so greatly is that everywhere, patent to everybody, in the simplest family life, there is proof of this truth. A man amuses himself skipping stones: the occupation has a pleasure hardly to be detected; with a wife it is interesting, with children it becomes exciting. Every new sharer adds to the father's stock of delight, so that at last he lies awake on winter nights thinking of the summer's pleasure. With a slight application of logic, democrats have struggled, and continually do struggle, to break down all the bastions, walls, and fences that time, prejudice, and ignorance have erected between men. They wish to have a ready channel from man to man, through which the emotional floods of life can pour ;

> "For they, at least,
> Have dream'd [that] human hearts might blend
> In one, and were through faith released
> From isolation without end."

The brotherhood of man, however, is not a week-day matter; men are brothers only in brief moments of poetry and enthusiasm; at other times they are unneighborly enough. The course of our civilization (so we are pleased to designate the aggregate of our incivil ways and habits) has helped the separation of man from man, not without excuse. Humanity has had a hard task in civilizing itself; in periods of ignorance, ill humor, and hunger it has built up a most elaborate system, which has been a great factor in material prosperity. This system is the specialization of labor, which serves to double the necessary differences among men, and to make every specialty and every difference a hindrance to the joys that should be in commonalty spread. The age of machinery has increased specialization, specialization has increased wealth, wealth is popularly supposed to be the panacea for human ills; and the bars and barriers between men have been repaired and strengthened. Specialization in Thackeray's time was in the very air; everything was specialized, — trade was specialized, society was specialized, money was specialized; there was money made, money inherited from father, money inherited from grandfather,—money, like blood, growing purer and richer the further back it could be traced. Every act of specialization produced a new batch of social relations.

To this elaborate system of specialization, and to its dividing properties, Thackeray is very sensitive. He has no gift for abstraction ; he does not take a man and grow absorbed in him as a spiritual being, as a creature in relations with some Absolute ; he sees men shut off and shut up in all sorts of little coops. He is all attentive to the coops. The world to him is one vast zoölogical garden, this Vanity Fair of his. He is not interested in the great concerns of life which make men cleave to one another, but in the different occupations, clothes, habits, which separate them into different groups. A democrat does not care for such classification ; on the contrary, he wishes to efface it as much as possible. He wishes to abstract man from his conditions and surroundings, and contemplate him as a certain quantity of human essence. He looks upon the distinctions of rank, of occupation, of customs and habits, as so many barricades upon the great avenues of human emotions ; Napoleon-like, he would sweep them away. He regards man as a serious reality, and these accidents of social relations as mere shadows passing over. This is the Christian position. This is the attitude of Victor Hugo, George Eliot, George Sand, Hawthorne, Tourgenef, Tolstoï, Charlotte Brontë.

No wonder that Charlotte Brontë made this criticism upon Thackeray's face: "To me the broad brow seems to express intellect. Certain lines about the nose and cheek betray the satirist and cynic; the mouth indicates a childlike simplicity, — perhaps even a degree of irresoluteness, inconsistency, — weakness, in short, but a weakness not unamiable. . . . A certain not quite Christian expression." This is a true likeness. Thackeray was not a Christian. He acted upon all the standards which Christianity has proclaimed to be false for nearly two thousand years. He had a certain childlike simplicity. Some of his best passages proceed upon it. Take the chapters in "Vanity Fair" where Amelia is neglected by Osborne, or the scene at Colonel Newcome's death. These incidents are described as they would appear to a child. The impressions seem to have been

dinted on the sensitive, inexperienced mind
of a child. This quality is Thackeray's
highest. He is able to throw off the dust
of years, and see things with the eyes of a
child, — not a child trailing glory from the
east, but one bred in healthful ignorance.

Walter Bagehot, in his essay on Sterne
and Thackeray, compares the two, and, after
describing Sterne's shiftless, lazy life, asks,
What can there be in common between him
and the great Thackeray, industrious and
moral? Bagehot found that the two had
sensitiveness in common. There is another
likeness, — a certain lack of independence, a
swimming with the stream. Thackeray has
an element of weakness; it appears continually in his method of writing novels. He
puts his character before you, but he never
suffers you to consider it by yourself; he is
nervously suggesting this and that; he is
afraid that you may misjudge what he con-
ceives to be his own correct moral standard.
He points out how virtuous he really is, how
good and noble. He keeps underscoring the
badness of his bad people, and the weakness
of his weak people. He is like a timid
mother, who will not let her brood out of

sight while any one is looking at them. Moreover, his satire never attacks anybody or anything that a man could be found publicly to defend. He charges upon social malefactors who are absolutely defenseless. He belabors brutality, avarice, boorishness, knavery, prevarication, with most resounding thwacks.

In the year 1847 "Vanity Fair" was published. Thackeray won great fame as the terrible satirist of society. And what did society do? Society invited him to dinner, in the correct belief that it and Thackeray agreed at every point. We think that such satire betrays a certain weakness and lack of courage. Did the Jesuits invite Molière to dinner after "Tartuffe"?

Thackeray's face had, according to the criticism we have quoted, "a weakness not unamiable." Certainly Thackeray was not unamiable; he must have been most lovable in many ways. The childlike characteristic to which we have alluded is enough to prove that; and in chapter after chapter we find evidence of his human kindliness. Take, for example, the passage quoted by Mr. Merivale, in his somewhat pugnacious Life of Thackeray, from Titmarsh's letter on Napoleon's funeral at Les Invalides. Here is a description of an English family in three generations, a somewhat foolish family, perhaps, given with some affectation, but perfectly genuine in its sympathy with childish hopes and fears. His books are full of passages of a like character. If further evidence were needed, Mrs. Ritchie's prefaces to this new edition supply it most abundantly.

VII

A novelist, however, in the end, must be judged according to a common human measure. This the novelist, like other men devoted to special pursuits, resents ; he interposes a claim of privilege, and demands a trial by his peers. He claims that as a man he may be judged by Tom, Dick, and Harry, but as a novelist — in that noble and sacrosanct capacity — he is only within the jurisdiction of men acquainted with the difficulties and triumphs of his art. This is the old error, — the Manichean heresy of trying to divide the one and indivisible into two. It reminds one of Gibbon's " I sighed as a lover, I obeyed as a son." It is the char-

acter of the novelist that provides tissue for
his novels; there is no way by which the
novelist can sit like an absentee god and project into the world a work that tells no tales
of him.   Every man casts his work in his
own image.   Only a great man writes a great
novel ; only a mean man writes a mean novel.
A novel is as purely a personal thing as a
handshake, and is to be judged by a simple
standard which everybody can understand.

There has been a foolish confusion of
nomenclature, due to the desire of critics to
make a special vocabulary for themselves,
partly to the end that they may be known
to be critics, partly to shut themselves off
into a species of the literary genus that shall
be judged only by members of the same
species.   Hence the silly words " idealism "
and " realism." Maupassant says : " How
childish it is to believe in reality, since each
of us carries his own in his mind !   Our eyes,
ears, noses, tastes, create as many different va-
rieties of truth as there are men in the world.
And we who receive the teachings of these
senses, affected each in his own way, analyze,
judge, and come to our conclusions as if we
all were of different races.   Each creates an

illusion of the world for himself, poetical, sentimental, gay, melancholy, ugly, or sad, according to his nature." This is a correct statement, but it does not go far enough. The world not only looks different to different people, but, as it is the most delicately plastic and sensitive matter imaginable, it is always tending to become for any community what the man in that community with the greatest capacity for expression thinks it is. Like an old Polonius, the city, the village, or the household sees the world in shape like a camel, or backed like a weasel or a whale, according as the prince among them thinks. Consider a fashion in criticism or in dress. Sir Joshua Reynolds admired Annibale Carracci, and all the people who looked at pictures, in very truth, saw beautiful pictures by the great, glorious Annibale. A group of dressmakers and ladies of quality in Paris wear jackets with tight sleeves, and every city-bred woman in France, England, and America sees the beauty of tight sleeves and the hideousness of loose sleeves.

Strictly speaking, everything is real and everything is ideal. The world is but an aggregate of opinions. The man who sees

an ugly world is as pure an idealist as he
who sees a glorious orb rising like the sun.
The question for poor humanity is, Shall the
earth shine or float dead and dull through
eternity? Every man who sees it golden
helps to gild it ; every man who sees it leaden
adds to its dross.

Shall we look with Miranda?

> " O, wonder !
> How many goodly creatures are there here !
> How beauteous mankind is !   O brave new world,
> That has such people in 't ! "

Or with Timon ?

> " All is oblique;
> There 's nothing level in our cursed natures,
> But direct villany."

The novelist is on the same standing-ground
as another; only he has the greater influence, and therefore the greater responsibility.
This world and all which inherit it are a
dream ; "why not make it a nobler dream
than it is ? "

Before this great act of creation, the petty
details of the novelist's craft — plot, story,
arrangement, epigram, eloquence — drop off
like last year's leaves. These details will
always find individuals to study them, to admire them, to be fond of them. They will

have their reward, they add to the interest
of life, they fill the vacant niches in the rich
man's time, they embroider and spangle.
They quicken our wits, stimulate our lazy
attentions, spice our daily food, help us to
enjoy; but they must not divert our attention
from the great interest of life, the struggle
between rival powers for the possession of the
world.   It is a need common to us and to
those who shall come after us, that the world
suffer no detriment in our eyes.   We must
see what poets see; one cannot help but dog-
matize and say that it is base to believe the
world base.   We need faith; we cannot do
without the power of noble expectation.

> " Is that Hope Faith, that lives in thought
>   On comforts which this world postpones,
>   That idly looks on life and groans
> And shuns the lessons it has taught ;
>
> " Which deems that after threescore years,
>   Love, peace, and joy become its due,
>   That timid wishes should come true
> In some safe spot untouched by fears ?
>
> " Or has he Faith who looks on life
>   As present chance to prove his heart,
>   As time to take the better part,
> And stronger grow by constant strife ;

" Who does not see the mean, the base,
    But sees the strong, the fresh, the true,
    Old hearts, old homes forever new,
    And all the world a glorious place ;

" So bent that they he loves shall find
    This earth a home both good and fair,
    That he is careless to be heir
    To all inheritance behind ? "